D0869421

A Church on Mission:
an Intentional Response
to the Needs of the Eighties

compiled by Reginald M. McDonough

385

Convention Press

This book is the text for a course in the subject area Basic Church
Leadership in the Church Study Course

Dewey Decimal Classification Number: 262.7
Subject heading: CHURCH
Printed in the United States of America

Contributors

Bob Banks and other staff persons, Brotherhood Commission

Ray Conner and other staff persons, Church Recreation Department, Sunday School Board

Roy Edgemon and other staff persons, Church Training Department, Sunday School Board

Mancil Ezell and other staff persons, Church Media Library Department, Sunday School Board

A. R. Fagan and other staff persons, Stewardship Commission, Southern Baptist Convention

Joe Hinkle and other staff persons, Family Ministry Department, Sunday School Board

C. B. Hogue and other staff persons, Evangelism Section, Home Mission Board

LeRoy McClard and other staff persons, Church Music Department, Sunday School Board

Albert McClellan, associate executive director and director of program planning, Executive Committee, Southern Baptist Convention

Reginald M. McDonough and other staff persons, Church Administration Department, Sunday School Board

Harry Piland and other staff persons, Sunday School Department, Sunday School Board

F. Jack Redford and other staff persons, Church Extension Department, Home Mission Board

Bobbie Sorrill and other staff persons, Woman's Missionary Union

The Church Study Course

THE CHURCH STUDY COURSE consists of a variety of short-term credit courses for adults and youth and noncredit foundational units for children and preschoolers. The materials are for use in addition to the study and training curriculums made available to the churches on an ongoing basis.

Study courses and foundational units are organized into a system that is promoted by the Sunday School Board, 127 Ninth Avenue, North, Nashville, Tennessee 37234; by the Woman's Missionary Union, 600 North Twentieth Street, Birmingham, Alabama 35203; by the Brotherhood Commission, 1548 Poplar Avenue, Memphis, Tennessee 37104; and by the respective departments of the state conventions affiliated with the Southern Baptist Convention.

Study course materials are flexible enough to be adapted to the needs of any Baptist church. The resources are published in several different formats—textbooks of various sizes, workbooks, and kits. Each item contains a brief explanation of the Church Study Course.

Types of Study and Credit

Adults and youth can earn study course credit through individual or group study. Teachers of courses or of foundational units are eligible to receive credit.

1. Class Experience.—Group involvement with course material for the designated number of hours for the particular course. Study course credit requirements call for a person to read, view, or listen to the course material and to attend class sessions. A person who is absent from one or more sessions must complete the "Personal Learning Activities" or other requirements for the material missed.

5

2. Individual Study.—This includes reading, viewing, or listening to course material and completing the specified requirements for the course.

3. Lesson Course Study.—Parallel use of designated study course material during the study of selected units in church program organization periodical curriculum units. Guidance for credit appears in the selected periodical.

4. Institutional Study.—Parallel use of designated study course material during regular courses at educational institutions, including Seminary Extension Department courses. Guidance for this means of credit is provided by the teacher.

Credit is awarded for the successful completion of a course of study. This credit is granted by the Church Study Course Awards Office, 127 Ninth Avenue, North, Nashville, Tennessee 37234, for the participating agencies. Credit may be requested on the coupon in the book, or Form 151, "Church Study Course Credit Request, Revised 1975."

When credit is issued to a person on request, the Awards Office sends two copies of a notice of credit earned to the church. The duplicate copy of the credit slip should be filed by the study course clerk in the participant's record of training folder. The original should be given to the person who earned the credit. Accumulated credits are applied toward a specific leadership diploma or the Christian Development Diplomas, which are measures of learning, growth, development, and training.

Detailed information about the Church Study Course system of credits, diplomas, and record keeping is available from the participating agencies. Study course materials, supplementary teaching or learning aids, and forms for record keeping may be ordered from Baptist Book Stores.

The Church Study Course Curriculum
Credit is granted on those courses listed in the current copy of the *Church Materials Catalog* and the *Church Study Course Catalog*. When selecting courses or foundational units, the current catalogs should be checked to determine what study course materials are valid.

How to Request Credit for This Course

This book is the text for a course in the subject area: Basic Church Leadership.

This course is designed for five hours of group study. Credit is awarded for attending class sessions and reading the book. A person who is absent from one or more class sessions must complete the "Personal Learning Activities" for the material missed.

Credit is also allowed for use of this material in individual study and, if so designated, in lesson course study and in institutional study.

A person desiring credit for individual study should read this book and complete the "Personal Learning Activities."

Credit for this study can be applied to one or more diplomas in the Church Study Course.

After the course is completed, the teacher, the study course clerk, the learner, or any person designated by the church should complete Form 151 (Church Study Course Credit Request, Revised 1975) and send it to the Awards Office, 127 Ninth Avenue, North, Nashville, Tennessee 37234. On the next page is a form which the reader may cut out, fill in, and send to the Awards Office for credit.

INSTRUCTIONS: If requested by the teacher, fill in this form and give it to him when the course is completed. If preferred, mail this request for course credit to

AWARDS OFFICE
THE SUNDAY SCHOOL BOARD, SBC
127 NINTH AVENUE, NORTH
NASHVILLE, TENNESSEE 37234

State Convention	Association	Indicate Type of Study (X)
		☐ Class ☐ Individual ☐ Lesson Course ☐ Educational Institution

CHURCH

Church Name _____

Mailing Address _____

City, State, Zip Code _____

MAIL TO

Mail to (If Different from Church Address)

Street, Route, or P.O. Box

City, State, Zip Code

LAST NAME	FIRST NAME AND MIDDLE INITIAL	MRS. (X)	COURSE TITLE
			A Church on Mission: an Intentional Response to the Needs of the Eighties

Cut along this line

Preface

The purpose of a church is dictated by God but the mission of a church is how a church interprets its God-given purpose in its setting. Each church has a unique mission. This is true because the gifts and opportunities of every church are different. Unfortunately tradition dulls the sensitivity of many churches to their mission. "We have always done it that way" is their guiding principle. These churches seem unaware of the changing world around them.

As the pace of change quickens in today's world, churches must increasingly ask themselves the questions: Why are we here? What must we be and do? How can we best achieve the peculiar mission of this church?

The purpose of this book is to give guidance to churches who are asking questions and to awaken in other churches the need to seriously consider the validity of these questions.

The eighties are projected to be equally as dynamic as the seventies.

The changing attitudes and mores, the shortage of energy, the high rate of inflation, the shift of population, and the changing sizes of the various age groups are bound to impact greatly the life and work of churches. Business as usual in churches will not keep pace with the everchanging scene of the decade to come. Churches must seek to know and pursue their unique mission. The subtitle of this volume is a mandate that shouts for attention—not just business as usual but a church program that responds intentionally to the needs of the eighties.

The first two chapters are foundational. To be on mission a church must understand its biblical foundations and the basic needs of persons. Chapter 3 seeks to survey the situation facing churches in the next decade. This chapter is a reprint of an article that appeared in the Winter 1980 issue of *Search*. The material is a condensation of a more detailed report that was prepared by O. D. Morris and Albert McClellan after getting input from many persons across the Southern Baptist Convention.

Chapter 4 calls attention to three priority concerns—evangelism, family ministry, and Christian discipleship. These concerns are being used by Southern Baptist Convention agencies as a major focus for the first half of the decade.

Chapter 5 presents a plan of organization to respond to the needs and priorities of the new decade. The statement of church tasks represents an updating of the listing of tasks that appeared in *A Dynamic Church: Spirit and Structure for the Seventies*, W. L. Howse and W. O. Thomason (1969, Convention Press).

Chapters 6-11 present a detailed explanation of the basic, service, and emphasis programs.

"Putting It Together with a Church Council," the final chapter, shows how a church can coordinate its many programs into a single thrust. Only then can a church expect to be optimally effective in the achievement of its mission.

A final reminder! A church cannot be and do the will of God unless it is willing to submit its life and work to the leadership of the Holy Spirit. Otherwise, a church will lack the power to relate meaningfully and triumphantly to its world.

I pray God's richest blessings on your church as under his leadership you seek to know and follow his will.

Reginald M. McDonough

Contents

Chapter 1

Biblical Foundations of a Church on Mission

The Bible contains truths and principles about the nature and work of a church. The biblical insights may be termed biblical foundations. A thorough study and understanding of these foundations is absolutely necessary if a church is to be on God's mission in the world. The Bible tells a church who it is and what it should be and do. As a foundation for developing a church program that is intentional and dynamic, this first chapter will present a brief look at the nature and functions of a church.

The biblical records offer no fixed patterns of church organization and prescribe no fixed methods of operation. In the freedom of the Spirit, the church explores and uses those techniques and methods most suitable for communicating the gospel and implementing the ministry Christ gave his people to perform.

THE NATURE OF THE CHURCH

Within the New Testament several descriptive terms set in focus the essential nature of the church.

1. The Church as the People of God

The word for church in the New Testament is *ekklesia*. In the Septuagint, the Greek translation of the Old Testament, this word translates the Hebrew term *qahal*. There the term referred to the nation Israel assembled before God, and so designated the people of God under divine rule (Deut. 31:30). *Ekklesia*, derived from the Greek verb *ekkaleo*, means "the called out ones." Among the Greeks, this meant an assembly of the people called out from their homes into some public place for the purpose of deliberating.

Organizational and institutional developments do not belong to the essential idea of *ekklesia*. These are, however, fairly indispensable for the life and work of the *ekklesia* in the world. For while *ekklesia* is general and inclusive of all those redeemed by Christ and made one in the family of God, the New Testament most frequently refers to the *ekklesia* as a local body, a fellowship of baptized believers, voluntarily associated with one another for worship, nurture, and service.

2. Other Biblical Descriptions of the Church

Biblical writers use several terms to describe the nature of the church.

Church of God.—"The church of God" (1 Cor. 1:2; 10:32; 11:22; 15:9; 2 Cor. 1:1; Gal. 1:13; 1 Tim. 3:5) or "the churches of God" (1 Cor. 11:16; 1 Thess. 2:14; 2 Thess. 1:4) reflects the idea that the church belongs to the Lord himself (Acts 20:28; Matt. 16:18).

People of God.—The church is sometimes called "the people of God," signifying a fellowship of persons, made one under God's kingly rule. W. T. Conner contends that the church "grew out of the redemptive mission and work of Jesus Christ" and should not be identified with the Old Testament order of things.[1] In describing "the people of God in Christ," however, New Testament writers use terms that were originally applied to Israel, the people associated with God's redemptive purpose. The church is "the Israel of God" (Gal. 6:16), "Abraham's offspring" (Gal. 3:29), "a chosen race, a royal priesthood, a holy nation, God's own people" (1 Pet. 2:9; see Ex. 19:6).

A family.—In a sense the church is like a family. Its members have been called into an intimate fellowship with Jesus, more binding than one's relationship to an earthly family (Matt. 10:37). Christ's true family consists of those who do the will of God (Mark 3:33-35); persons who have obeyed the summons to leave all and follow him (Mark 1:17-20; 2:14; 8:34; 10:21; Luke 9:23,59; John 1:43; 10:27; 12:26).

Branch or vine.—The church is related to Christ as fruitful branches are related to a vine (John 15:1-8). Jesus drew on the Old Testament symbols that depicted Israel as a vine or a vineyard (Ps. 80:8-13; Isa. 5:1-7; Jer. 2:21; Hos. 9:10). "I am the vine, you are the branches."

God's flock.—The people of God, in the Old Testament, are sometimes described as God's flock (Isa. 40:11; Ps. 23). Jesus used the same terminology in referring to his followers (Matt. 26:31; Luke 12:32; John 10:16; 21:15:17).

Body of Christ.—Paul most frequently describes the church as "the body of Christ" (Rom. 12:4-5; 1 Cor. 12:12-27; Eph. 1:22-23; 2:14-16; 3:3-13; 4:1-16; 5:30; Col. 1:18, 24; 2:16-19; 3:15). From his statements we may draw several pertinent conclusions:

• Jesus Christ is the head, and the only head, of the church.

• The members of the church are members because of their intimate relationship with him.

• The purpose of the body of Christ is to carry out the will of its divine head.

• Like the members of the physical body, church members, individually and collectively, have a wide variety of responsibilities to carry out.

• Each member has his own particular and individual gifts, yet all members are interrelated and need one another.

Although the members have various gifts, there is real and vital unity in the body of Christ.

God's field.—The church is "God's field" (1 Cor. 3:9), like a garden plot under God's cultivation for the purpose of bearing fruit for his glory.

God's building.—The church is "God's building" (1 Cor. 3:9), being constructed according to his plan. In the same chapter (1 Cor. 3:16), the church is described as a temple or sanctuary. God builds his church out of living persons redeemed by his grace. The result is "a spiritual house" (1 Pet. 2:5) wherein God is pleased to dwell. And his presence makes possible and necessary a "holy" people (1 Cor. 3:17).

Fellowship of believers.—The church is a fellowship of believers empowered by the Holy Spirit. The distinctive word for fellowship is *koinonia*. This term means sharing, participation, communion, fellowship. *Koinonia* is not a human creation. It is the gift of God, the product of relationship with him (1 John 1:3).

New humanity.—In the Pauline letters, the church is pictured as a "new humanity." This new humanity is God's creation through Christ and consists of diverse groups heretofore set against one another (Eph. 2:14-20; Gal. 6:15).

Bride of Christ.—Reminiscent of the Old Testament prophets who used domestic figures to depict the relation of Israel and Jehovah (Hos. 2:1-17; Isa. 54:1-10; Ps. 45), the New Testament writers refer to the church as the bride of Christ (2 Cor. 11:2-3; Eph. 5:25-32; Rev. 19:7-9; 21:9). The Gospels complete the analogy by depicting Christ as a bridegroom (Matt. 22:2; 25:1-13; Mark 2:18-20; Luke 14:7-11; John 3:25-29). As with a wholesome marital relationship, the relationship between Christ and his people is one of love and fidelity.

Pillar of the truth.—The "church of the living God" is also the pillar and bulwark of the truth (1 Tim. 3:15). The words *pillar* and *bulwark* designate the church as key witness to the truth of God's revelation. They also suggest the church's role in supporting and defending the truth both verbally and nonverbally (1 Pet. 3:15-16; Jude 3; 1 Tim. 4:13).

3. A Divine Institution

The church is a divine institution. The New Testament fully substantiates this claim.

According to the biblical record, the church originated in the mind of God and was created to serve his purposes.

The church is divine in its relationships. First, there is its relationship to God. Those who form the "spiritual temple" are God's people. First Peter 2:4-10 grounds the doctrine of the priesthood of all believers in this divine ownership.

Second, the church is divine because of its relationship to Jesus Christ, the founder and head of the church (Matt. 16:18; Col. 1:18; Eph. 1:22-23; 4:15; 5:23). In that unique relationship the church is like a body to the head (1 Cor. 6:15 f.; 10:14-22; 11:28 f.; 12:12,14; Rom. 7:4; 12:5; Col. 1:24; 3:15) and must function as the head desires.

Third, though the church belongs to God, and Jesus Christ is its founder and head, there is a sense in which the Holy Spirit brought the church into existence. And it is the Holy Spirit by whose power the church maintains its life and growth.

THE PURPOSE OF THE CHURCH

The purpose of the church is to carry out the will of Christ in the world, to proclaim and apply his gospel. This involves worship, proclamation and witness, nurture and education, and ministry.

1. Worship

The early church, following the example of Jesus (Luke 4:16), met regularly for worship and provided instruction concerning worship. Immediately following Pentecost, the church engaged in worship daily (Acts 2:46). Places of worship varied: Temple, synagogue, or homes of believers. Later, regular meetings of the Christian fellowship occurred on the first day of the week (Acts 20:7; 1 Cor. 16:2).

Worship is encountering God in experiences that deepen a Christian's faith and strengthens his service. W. T. Conner writes that "the worship of God in Christ should be at the center of all else the church does. It is the mainspring of all the activity of the church."[2]

2. Proclamation and Witness

The entire church is responsible for proclamation and witness. Jesus came preaching, calling for repentance and obedience to God's kingly rule (Mark 1:14). One of his first acts was to call out followers who would share this mission (Mark 1:16-20). He not only taught his disciples essential truths but he sent them out to proclaim the kingdom of God and to give witness to the compassion and power of the Father (Matt. 10:5-15; Mark 6:7-13; Luke 9:1-6; 10:1-18). After his resurrection, he commissioned them to be witnesses of the good news of God's saving act, to make disciples everywhere, and to ground new converts in his teaching (Luke 24:46-48; Matt. 28:19-20; John 20:21).

For this task, the disciples were to receive power through the Holy Spirit (Acts 1:8; 10:42). The book of Acts shows the early church empowered and guided by the Spirit, faithfully giving witness to the living Lord and proclaiming God's judgment on sin and his mercy for sinners (Acts 1:22; 2:4; 3:15; 4:33). The entire church was caught up in this proclamation and witness though special attention focuses upon notable leaders like Peter and John (Acts 2:14-41; 3:1-26; 5:42; 8:4).

3. Nurture and Education
Nurture and education includes the whole process by which the church prepared persons for the acceptance of Christ, and after conversion guided their development toward the goals of Christian maturity. Nurture and education are the two sides of one coin. Nurture is the sum of experiences that nourish, modify, and develop individuals within a fellowship. Education involves the means provided for growth in knowledge, wisdom, moral righteousness, and performance. The nurturing process suggests a protective guardianship; the educating process is designed to produce maturity. Both are concerned for the development of competent, full-grown persons who can themselves share the nurturing, educating task.

There is evidence that the early churches took seriously Jesus' command to "teach disciples" (Matt. 28:20). Disciples are developed through teaching, the discovery and use of spiritual gifts, the development of skills, and a lifetime of obedience. Careful students of the New Testament are convinced that the churches carefully instructed new converts in the faith, following a simple pattern of teaching (Acts 2:42; 1 Cor. 15:1-7; 2 Thess. 2:15). The New Testament church was a teaching, nurturing community.

Believers were expected to grow in grace and knowledge toward full maturity in Christ (2 Pet. 3:18; Eph. 4:11-13). While individuals were responsible for their Christian growth and action (2 Tim. 2:15; 2 Pet. 1:5-11), the church was enjoined to cultivate these. Church leaders had the task of feeding the flock (John 21:15-17; 1 Pet. 5:2; Acts 20:28), and the pastor-teacher had heavy responsibility for "equipping the saints for ministry" (Eph. 4:11).

Church growth, as the New Testament discloses, is both numerical and spiritual. What we call nurture is related to both, especially the second. The church is built up from within through

18

education and nurture, unity in worship, fellowship, and the cultivation and proper use of spiritual gifts (Acts 2:41-47). A low level of spiritual development evoked censure from church leaders and accounts for some of the strongest admonitions in the existing records (1 Cor. 3:1-4; Gal. 4:1-20; Heb. 5:12-6:3). The transmission of the gospel itself called for the development of faithful witnesses (2 Tim. 2:2).

4. Ministry

The church receives its ministry from Jesus Christ. He is forever the example of sacrificial, self-giving love. He "went about doing good" (Acts 10:38), ministering to human need, challenging abuses of power, instructing his followers to forget themselves and give themselves in a gracious service to others (Matt. 20:25-28; John 13:15). The ministry to which Christ calls his followers takes many forms (Matt. 25:34-40), but its distinctiveness rests in the fact that it is done in his name and for his glory. Our ministry (*diakonia*) is always by the mercy of God (2 Cor. 4:1) and it must reflect the spirit of Christ.

The church's ministry involves practical acts—Christians helping Christians who are in need. It also involves the church, individually and collectively, in doing "good to all men" (Gal. 6:10). Following Jesus' example the church seeks to minister to the whole person. This means a concern for the spiritual, mental, and physical welfare of persons, both within and without the church (Acts 3:6; 6:1-6; 16:16-18; 19:11-12; Rom. 15:25-27). "Faith working through love" makes us "servants of one another" (Gal. 5:6, 13). This spirit in us leads to "good works and acts of charity" (Acts 9:36). True ministry in Christ's name calls for positive action, not mere verbal exercises (Jas. 2:14-17).

THE BASIC INTENTIONS OF A CHURCH

New Testament teachings of the church seem to indicate that a church's work—and hence its objectives—falls into three areas: the making of vital Christian disciples, the fostering of members' growth toward Christian maturity, and the development of spiritual power in the lives of its members.

19

1. Make Christian Disciples

The command to make disciples is at the heart of the Great Commission (Matt. 28:19-20). Vital Christian discipleship begins with an authentic salvation experience. It includes daily self-denial and commitment to the lordship of Jesus Christ (Mark 8:34; Luke 9:23). The disciple is a *learner* (Matt. 11:29)—that is the meaning of the word itself. But disciples are also *doers*. Obedience to Christ is the very essence of discipleship (Luke 6:46).

Disciples are called upon to share the Master's life and work (Matt. 10:24-25), to be self-giving and sacrificial; to be "out of this world" (John 17:14-17; Col. 3:2), yet lovingly attentive to its aching hurts and needs. Disciples, so Jesus said, must bear a cross. His meaning is clear: unconditional surrender to the will of God regardless of the risks involved.

2. Help Members Grow

The church seeks to develop its members toward the goal of Christian maturity. Jesus urged perfection like that of God the Father (Matt. 5:48). From the context it appears that he was referring to a love that was impartial and benevolent. Biblical writers, dealing with Christian growth and patterns of maturity, invariably include the expansion and expression of love (1 Thess. 4:9-10; 2 Thess. 1:3; Phil. 1:9-11; Eph. 3:17-19; Heb. 13:1; 1 John 4:7-21). They also look for the enlargement of faith (2 Thess. 1:3), spiritual insight and wisdom (Col. 1:9-10; James 1:5), the discipline of the flesh (Gal. 5:16-21,24), and the development of a disposition and character after the example of Jesus.

3. Cultivate Spiritual Power

Every church should seek for maximum moral and spiritual power in the lives of its members and in the body of the church as a whole. Powerless Christians and weak churches indicate the absence of the Holy Spirit, who is our source of energy. Jesus foresaw his followers engaged in extensive labors (John 14:12) and promised the power of the Spirit as they sought to accomplish their God-given mission (Acts 1:8). The coming of the Spirit released the church for its task and undergirded it for effective witnessing (Acts 2:4).

FOUNDATIONS FOR CHURCH ORGANIZATION

From the available records we find certain principles of church organization:

- Each church is an autonomous spiritual body under the leadership of Christ.
- All members have equal rights and privileges in the church. (This principle is rooted in the fundamental Christian doctrine of the priesthood of all believers.)
- Each member ought to be meaningfully involved in the functioning of his church (Rom. 12:4-8; 1 Cor. 12).
- Organization should be suited to needs and situations as they develop.
- Organizations must serve the purposes of the church.
- Churches are interdependent with other New Testament churches for mutual support and effort.

The New Testament church started out with no prescribed organizational structure. It was usually organized around local needs.

This absence of a fixed pattern has led modern scholars (depending on their bias) to see in the records traces of different forms of church government. Baptists in general agree that the evidence points strongly to a congregational pattern.

Apparently there was never more than one church organization in a given locality. There was, for example, just one church at Jerusalem, one at Corinth, one at Rome, one at Ephesus, one at Philippi. The words *churches in Galatia* designate churches in a province, not in a city.

The question naturally arises, "Where did a huge congregation such as that at Jerusalem hold its meetings?" Some scholars feel that churches divided their memberships into small groups with each group meeting in a different location. The Jerusalem church with its thousands of members (Acts 4:4), in the absence of an available facility large enough to house its congregation, would have had small groups gathering in several different places.

We should remember that the Spirit of God is at work within the churches today. He may lead us to create new structures to meet developing needs. This can mean a variety of patterns even when a common faith is shared. Each congregation must be free to determine its pattern of organization in keeping with a Bible-based and Spirit-guided understanding of its mission.

FOUNDATIONS FOR CHURCH RELATIONSHIPS

Each local church exists in a network of relationships.

1. Internal Relationships

There are internal relationships. Church members have individual functions, but they are mutually dependent, each needing the others. Accordingly, there must be a division of labor. The Jerusalem church illustrates this principle of operation in its decision to separate the function of proclamation and worship from that of practical ministry. The selection of seven "laymen" for the latter function left the apostles free to assume the proclamation and worship duties. The church, so Paul noted, best fulfills its mission and ministry when each member exercises his gifts and does his share of the work (Rom. 12:4-12; 1 Cor. 12; Eph. 4:11-16).

Internal relationships can be disrupted by immaturities, selfishness, and misguided zeal. The Corinthian church is an example here. But the example and the spirit of Jesus and the love which he commanded (John 13:1-15; 15:34-35) point a better way for the church. The New Testament letters are filled with admonitions concerning Christian attitudes and behavior. These call for mutual respect among members, mutual helpfulness, mutual forbearance, joint efforts for harmony, and sincere forgiveness.

2. Relationship with Other Churches

The New Testament gives guidance concerning interchurch relationships. The threat of a common problem or need brought representatives of churches together for discussion and action.

Acts 15 presents a record of the first council of churches. There the issue centered upon the nature of salvation itself. One group, led by Paul, contended for a gospel of free grace. The other, made up of Judaizers, insisted that Gentile converts should subscribe to certain Jewish rites and customs. After considerable discussion the council worked out a compromised statement which was sent out to the churches (Acts 15:22-31).

Second, interchurch cooperation was sometimes a response to human need. A notable example is the special offering which the Gentile churches raised for the relief of the poor at Jerusalem. Paul and his colleagues directed this work of benevolence.

Another way in which New Testament churches jointly shared responsibilities was in the entertaining of visiting preachers and members (3 John 5-6; Rom. 12:13; Heb. 13:2; Titus 3:13). The ancient world lacked adequate public lodging places, and Christians generally lacked expense money. Christian love encouraged hospitality. Itinerant churchmen both received and bestowed blessings when admitted to a household.

There is no indication that interchurch relationship ever caused a congregation to lose its independence or autonomy. Despite the apostle Paul's frequent assertions of apostolic authority, he never coerced any church to participate in the cooperative offering which he collected. There is no indication that any church or combination of churches imposed regulations upon other congregations.

3. Relationship to Society

Churches exist within a secular society and always have some kind of relationship to it. In the New Testament records, the church is in tension with the "world" (society in alienation from God, often radically opposed to him). Christians live in the world but they are "not of the world" (John 17:14-16). The contrasts between the Christian community and the world are sharply drawn (Eph. 2:1-13), and believers are enjoined neither to love the world (1 John 2:15-17) nor to conform to its standards and life-styles (Rom. 12:2).

Christian lives, therefore, are markedly different from the

lives of nonbelievers. But Christians live within the world, not in monastic withdrawal from it. To be an effective force in society, the church must understand its relationship to that society. That relationship never means an isolation from the world.

Efforts for the salvation of others constitute the major responsibility of a New Testament church to the world about it. The Holy Spirit repeatedly led New Testament churches to make a definite outreach for people in the name of the Lord (Acts 13:1-3; 14:26-27; Phil. 4:10-18; 3 John 5:8).

In addition to direct efforts to win persons to faith in Christ, the church should also take a positive stand for righteousness and work earnestly to bring about mutual respect, brotherhood, justice, and peace in all the relationships of men and races and nations. It confidently works and waits for the ultimate fulfillment of God's purpose for the world.

4. Relationship to the State

A pattern for church-state relationships begins to emerge in the New Testament. This begins with a recognition that the institution of civil government possesses divine origin. Paul went so far as to say that there is no governing authority except from God, and those that exist have been instituted by God (Rom. 13:1). Both church and state have been instituted by God and both are answerable to him. Each is distinct in purpose and function, as we may readily infer from Jesus' famous saying, "Render to Caesar the things that are Caesar's, and to God the things that are God's" (Mark 12:17; Matt. 22:21; Luke 20:25). The early Christians were taught not only to pray for the civil authorities but also to obey them where no violation of conscience was concerned.

All of this accords with Jesus' teaching. The principle underlying his commandment to pay tribute to Caesar was that persons who benefited by the advantages which Caesar provided owed Caesar a proportionate share of the cost of such benefits. Implied also is the fact that church and state are to remain separate but are to stand in proper relationship with each other under God.

---

1. W. T. Conner, *Christian Doctrine* (Nashville: Broadman Press, 1937), p. 259.
2. W. T. Conner, *The Gospel of Redemption* (Nashville: Broadman Press, 1945), p. 277.

Chapter 2

Examining the Basic Needs of Persons

The life and work of a church is aimed at the salvation and growth of persons. The needs of persons should be the targets that give direction and priority to a church's efforts. An intentional ministry must be aimed at meeting the needs of persons. The needs of persons provide the focus of a church's life and work as it carries out its God-given purpose.

Needs are the mainsprings of human behavior. A need may be defined as a drive, motive, urge, desire, or instinct that causes persons to act as they do. A need may be a push caused by a deficit or it may be a pull caused by a goal or desire. Although psychology has taught us a lot about the needs of persons, the insights derived from biblical principles provide the best backdrop for an understanding of human needs.

THE SPIRITUAL NATURE AND NEEDS OF PERSONS

"When I look at thy heavens, the work of thy fingers, the moon and the stars which thou has established; what is man that thou art mindful of him, and the son of man that thou doest care for him? Yet thou hast made him little less than God, and doest crown him with glory and honor. Thou has given him dominion over the work of thy hands; thou hast put all things under his feet, all sheep and oxen, and also the beast of the field, the birds of the air, and the fish of the sea, whatever passes along the paths of the sea. O Lord, our Lord, how majestic is thy name in all the earth!" (Ps. 8:3-8, RSV).[1]

This and many other references in the Scriptures make it clear that the peak of God's creative activity was the creation of a person, a human being made in his own likeness.

1. A Sense of Worth
Although the worth of the minerals in the human body is only

a few dollars, the value of a person is priceless in God's sight. Since God places persons in such high esteem, it follows that he expects his children to hold themselves in the highest esteem. He also expects individuals to treat one another as persons of great worth.

The crown of God's creation.—Scientists have provided invaluable data in understanding God's creation—the human personality. It is important to understand all this data. But it would be foolish to attempt to formulate a Christian philosophy of persons without first considering the biblical view of the peak of God's creation.

God's creatve process reached its zenith in the creation of man. The earlier verses of Genesis 1 tell of God's creation of the heavenly bodies, the earth, the plants, the animals, the birds, and the fish. At each stage of creation, God said that it was good. But when God created man and woman, he went beyond such an expression. He gave them dominion over the earth and everything in it.

The image of God.—As if it weren't enough to give man and woman a place at the apex of creation, God created them in his own image. Genesis 1:27 records that "God created man in His own image, in the image of God He created him: male and female He created them" (NASB).[2]

What does it mean to be created in the image of God? Are we physically like God? William Hendricks explains the view held by many scholars: "If God were physical as we are, how could he be present in all times and places (Ps. 139)? Christian theology must not picture people as puppets cut from a master pattern of a physical God. Nor can we image God as a vision of a human drawn to a larger scale. A more acceptable view of the image of God in man is that the image is in a person's reasoning ability."[3]

The ability to reason is a major asset that sets human beings apart from God's other creation. The Scriptures say; "Come now and let us reason together" (Isa. 1:18).

The uniqueness of gifts. —God is the creator not just of mankind as a species but of every individual person. He has created every person as an original being with definite and unique gifts. The followers of Christ have been given gifts and these are given for the "equipping of the saints . . . to the building up of the body of Christ" (Eph. 4:12, NASB). A gift is a concrete and personal realization of grace in the life of the believer. Through these gifts people discover the essence and purpose of their lives. It is through the use of the gifts God has given persons that he continues his creative work.

2. The Meaning of Image

Relationship to God's image is also seen in the emotional, rational, and social characteristics of persons. We are feeling beings. We are relating beings.

Emotional beings.—As emotional beings, men and women are capable of feeling. The ability to feel gives persons the capacity to love. Without this capacity to love, one could not relate meaningfully to self, to others, or to God. God is love—he is a feeling God. To respond to him, persons made in his image are also feeling beings.

Rational capacity.—The rational capacity of persons gives them the ability to exercise will. This capacity transcends the physical. It provides the ability to project meaning.

Social nature.—The social nature of persons gives them the ability to relate meaningfully to other God-created persons—to have fellowship with one another.

Persons of potential.—Persons created in the image of God have the potential to be a part of God's continuing creation in the world. And that potential is increased in persons who have been recreated into the image of Christ. Persons who are open to the leadership of God's Spirit and the resurrection power made available through Jesus Christ will realize continuing growth in all areas of their lives. Those who have been created in God's image and recreated in Christ are continually becoming. The boundaries of their potentials are always moving.

3. Endowed with Freedom of Choice

In the garden, Adam and Eve were given the freedom to choose how they would live, but they had a responsibility to obey God. Because they were responsible for their actions, they had to bear the consequences when they disobeyed God.

27

Self-determination.—Freedom means that in the human personality God did not make a puppet on a string to be pushed and pulled at will; each person has the freedom of self-determination. But with this freedom comes responsibility.

Mullins expressed this idea forcefully: "Freedom does not imply exemption from the operation of influences, motives, heredity, environment. It means rather that man is not under compulsion. His actions are in the last resort determined from within."[4]

Freedom and evil.—Persons have the freedom to choose good or evil. Otherwise a person's worship of God would be worthless. Love and adoration are meaningless if they do not arise out of free will. Although this privilege gives persons great opportunity, it carries with it both risk and responsibility. Each person must be responsible for his or her acts.

Jesus grieved over the city of Jerusalem, but he did not take responsibility for the people's behavior. That responsibility belonged to them, just as persons today are responsible for their behavior.

The act of marriage illustrates the concept of freedom and responsibility. In the United States, two adults are free to get married. They may exercise their freedom to do so. But when they enter this marriage relationship, a responsibility to the other partner must be assumed. If no commitment and no mutual responsibility exist, the relationship has no meaning; it will eventually fall apart. All meaningful relationships are build on the premise of mutual freedom and responsibility.

The ultimate decision about response to God springs from within each person. To obey God and allow him to use the highest of his creation is a decision that each person must make for himself.

4. Marred by Sin

Each person is created in the image of God, the crown of creation, with dominion over the earth. He is given the freedom to choose. But this is only part of the picture—the part that speaks to opportunity. There is more. Sin has marred this picture.

Disobedience is sin.—The biblical picture of persons is not complete without exploring how men and women have responded to their freedom. God created persons to have close fellowship with him. Genesis 3:8 implies that God had direct fellowship with Adam and Eve before they disobeyed him. That fellowship was based on a relationship of freedom and obedience. But Adam and Eve chose to disobey God. Thus, by their own choice, they disrupted the special relationship they had with God. They failed to live up to the full potential that God placed in them. From Genesis 3 to contemporary history, individuals have continued to use their freedom to disobey. Disobedience was and continues to be sin.

All have sinned.—In Romans 3:23, Paul wrote that "all have sinned." He did not outline the origin or the cause of sin; he simply stated the human condition. The fact is that all persons are sinners. Each person, on his own, has chosen to compete with God in ruling his creation. This ego-centered nature continues to be the basis of man's disobedience. Persons rebel against God and fall short of their potential. Each fallen person hides from God and seeks to blame other persons for that plight.

Evil causes suffering.—The dilemma of why persons suffer in a world ruled by an all-powerful and loving God can be explained in part by the exercise of free choice. "Our freedom" says William Hendricks, "has produced evil which causes both us and God to suffer. The step from innocence to responsibility involves both man and God. We have not carried the weight of our responsibility well."[5] While God has remained true to his responsibility for creation, he does not revoke his gift of choice. Thus evil continues to be present in the world and is the cause of much suffering.

5. Implications of Rebellion and Sin

Rebellion and sin have several implications regarding human behavior.

Individuals are not always predictable.—A human being is not a precisely predictable creature. He is influenced by both God and Satan. Paul said, "I am a mortal man, sold as a slave to sin. I do not understand what I do; for I don't do what I would like to do, but instead I do what I hate" (Rom. 7:15, GNB).[6] There is always a struggle within a person between the intention of God's creation and the human urge to disobey.

29

Persons are self-centered.—Another important aspect of the presence of sin in human lives is the effect of self-worship on behavior. Each person is turned inward. Most people give first priority to selfish needs and desires. It becomes easy to resort to manipulation of self and of others. Self-sacrifice is difficult.

Self-centeredness is not altogether negative. Some degree of self-centeredness may simply be self-esteem. It is this sense of self-worth that enables a person to celebrate his or her gifts and relate meaningfully to others. The Scriptures say: "Love your neighbor as yourself." Self-love, then, is a model for loving others. Only when a person carries that sense of self-worth to excess does it become harmful.

6. Redeemed by Love

"For sin pays its wage—death; but God's free gift is eternal life in union with Christ Jesus our Lord" (Rom. 6:23, GNB).

God exalted man and woman by creating them in his own image and by giving them dominion over the earth. He honored them by giving them the freedom to choose good or evil. But God in his foreknowledge was aware this relationship would be broken. So he took a further step. Out of that great love, God planned a way by which he could reclaim his fallen creation. Redemptive love made a way to restore the broken relationship between God and persons.

God's initiative.—God took the initiative to search out Adam and Eve after they had sinned. God's first communication was "Where are you?" (Gen. 3:9, GNB). This searching love has continued to be God's response to the rebellion of his sons and daughters.

In the Old Testament God provided a sacrificial system to make atonement for sin and remove the barrier between God and man. But atonement in the Old Testament always looked forward to the perfect sacrifice in Jesus Christ, in whom God demonstrated love that conquered sin and death. "God offered him, so that by his death he should become the means by which people's sins are forgiven through their faith in him" (Rom. 3:25, GNB).

Man's options.—Because of God's great love for all persons, he has made a way for each returning person to be forgiven. Thus he makes it possible for the fellowship that was marred by sin of self-will and rebellion to be restored. But God does not force his gifts on anyone. Each person has the option to accept or reject the love that God offers.

God's provision for restoring fellowship with this creation has given each person the capacity to rise above his self-centeredness and recapture in his or her personality the God-like traits of love and forgiveness. Sinful persons do respond to God's love. This gives meaning and purpose to the work of the church.

7. Reaffirmed by Jesus

Jesus not only made salvation possible but he also reaffirmed through his teachings the focus of God's love. Many of his parables and figures of speech illustrate God's love and care for all persons. Matthew recorded these words of Jesus: "Yet not one sparrow falls to the ground without your Father's consent. As for you, even the hairs of your head have all been counted. So do not be afraid; you are worth much more than many sparrows" (Matt. 10:29-31, GNB).

Jesus told the parable of the prodigal son who rejected his father's love and squandered his inheritance. But he was welcomed back to the father's household and restored to fellowship in the family. God, he said, is like a shepherd who, when one sheep is lost, leaves the other to find the one that has strayed.

8. Realized Through Community

God's ultimate purpose for redeemed persons is life in community with others. Christians do not realize their full potential as individuals in isolation from others. The growth of disciples is into a body—the body of Christ—the church. This growth into maturity comes when all members of the body are in their rightful places, utilizing their special gifts, and living under the lordship of Christ.

An ultimate goal of the Christian's life is the upbuilding of the church. Christ himself molds the members of his body together. The gifts, abilities, and capacities of one combined with others makes growth possible. "We are meant to hold firmly to the truth in love, and to grow up in every way into Christ the head. For it is

31

from the head that the whole body, as a harmonious structure knit together by the joints with which it is provided, grows by the proper functioning of individual parts to its full maturity" (Eph. 4:15-16, Phillips).[7]

OTHER BASIC NEEDS OF PERSONS

Basic needs are felt to some extent by all persons. These needs may be classified into five categories: physiological needs, safety needs, social needs, esteem needs, and growth needs.

1. Physiological Needs

Physiological needs are man's most basic needs. They are innate, biological needs which stimulate a person to preserve life and health. Every person, for example, needs food, water, rest, and oxygen. These are the strongest of the physiological needs.

Physiological needs are generally satisfied outside the church building. But such conveniences as meals, heating and air-conditioning, rest rooms, and water fountains are some of the ways that congregations acknowledge the motivational strengths of these needs.

2. Safety Needs

Safety needs are another category of needs that motivate persons. These needs generally emerge when a person's physiological needs are being met. These include the need for security, stability, dependence, and protection; freedom from fear, anxiety, and chaos; structure, order, law, limits, and strength in the protector.

Safety needs play a significant role in a person's decision to become a Christian. It is through a person's felt need for eternal security that the Holy Spirit often works to bring a person to repentance and faith.

A person's response to change is another area where safety needs come into play. Persons often prefer the familiar to the unfamiliar. For example, one reason many adults do not want to change Bible study classes as they grow older can be traced to their need for safety. The new environment may be a threat to their needs for stability, structure, and order. A wise church leader will seek to reduce the threat of instability when suggesting changes.

3. Social Needs

Persons are social beings. They need to love and be loved. They need to interact with other persons, to feel accepted, and to belong. Solitary confinement has long been regarded as the most severe punishment in the penal system short of death.

A person's social needs, however, go beyond obtaining love and avoiding loneliness. Giving affection is also a very significant aspect of a person's social needs. Giving and receiving are both important. This is particularly relevant to Christians. For them, giving is an important way of expressing the Christian faith.

There are many ways a church relates to this area of need. The church is a fellowship of believers where persons are united in the body of Christ. Many of the small-group activities of a church meet the fellowship needs of persons. The ways we reach out to others through ministries give opportunities for expressions of love.

The need for love and acceptance is universal. Until a person has experienced some measure of fulfillment of these needs, he cannot achieve the potential that God has placed in him.

4. Esteem Needs

All persons have a need for a stable, firmly based, high evaluation of themselves, for self-respect, for self-esteem, and for the esteem of others. The esteem needs can be divided into two categories: self-esteem and esteem for others.

Self-esteem.—Self-esteem includes such needs as the desire for confidence, competence, mastery, adequacy, achievement, independence, and freedom. Self-image is built on a person's self-esteem. A person's self-image is often a controlling factor in his happiness and achievement.

A person may be highly motivated until he reaches his perceived high-water mark in Christian development. At that point he ceases to grow because he has satisfied his self-image. A person's self-image seems to place an imaginary lid on his motivation to grow and develop.

At the same time, many persons are frustrated in their mid-years because they have accomplished all of their goals for family, education, etc.; but they have not achieved as much as they think they should. This is what is often referred to as the mid-career crisis. At this point persons have to shift emotionally from tangible goals to quality-of-life goals. This is not easy to do.

Esteem of others.—To have the esteem of others is the second category of esteem needs. Esteem from others includes the need for prestige, recognition, acceptance, attention, status, reputation, and appreciation. Each of us wants and needs to be appreciated by others. A person's self-esteem is largely built on the feedback that is received from others.

Esteem needs are intricately involved in a person's church life. Because the church and Christian leaders are important in the life of a Christian, the approval or rejection a person receives from them is highly significant to his self-esteem. Rejection by a minister is for many persons like rejection by God. For this reason, ministers have the power to bless or to curse.

5. Growth Needs

Within each person is the need to become all he can become. These needs emerge only after reasonable social and esteem needs are met.

The pursuit of a person's growth needs also appears to differ from that of other need areas. Physiological, safety, social, and esteem needs appear to operate in cycles. Each cycle begins with a deficit or disequilibrium. Out of this need a goal is set. Behavior is altered to reach the goal and the deficit is satisfied. These cycles operate hundreds of times each day. The key word is deficit. The deficit initiates the cycle.

Growth action, on the other hand, appears to stem not from a deficit but from a need to achieve and become. Some persons have high need for achievement. They tend to stretch themselves to become all their potential will allow.

The apostle Paul appears to have been strongly influenced by growth needs. In Philippians 3:14, he states, "I press toward the mark for the prize of the high calling of God in Christ Jesus." In Christian circles, the term *being on mission* is often used. This concept expresses the concept of stretching to become all that God has given the capacity to become and of directing that capacity toward the achievement of a worthy goal.

The many needs of human beings represent the pulls of life. None of the needs is more Christian than another. God made all of each of us. The Holy Spirit works through all aspects of our personality. Problems arise not because we have these God-given needs but because we try to meet these needs in our own way without seeking God's will and direction for our lives.

1. From the Revised Standard Version of the Bible, copyrighted 1946, 1952, © 1971, 1973.
2. From the *New American Standard Bible*. © The Lockman Foundation, La Habra, California, 1971. Published by Creation House, Inc., Carol Stream, Illinois. All succeeding quotations from this version are indicated by the abbreviation NASB in parentheses.
3. William L. Hendricks, *The Doctrine of Man* (Nashville: Convention Press, 1977), pp. 47-48.
4. E. Y. Mullins, *The Christian Religion in Its Doctrinal Expression* (Philadelphia: Judson Press, 1917), p. 255.
5. Hendricks, *The Doctrine of Man*.
6. This quotation is from the *Good News Bible,* the Bible in Today's English Version. Old Testament: Copyright © American Bible Society 1966, 1971, 1976. Used by permission. Subsequent quotations are marked GNB.
7. Reprinted with permission of Macmillian Publishing Co., Inc. from J. B. Phillips: *The New Testament in Modern English,* Revised Edition. © J. B. Phillips 1958, 1960, 1972.

Chapter 3

The Needs of the Eighties

About thirty years ago Kenneth Scott Latourette, the renowned Baptist church historian, wrote a book entitled *Tomorrow Is Here*. It was an attempt to show that history was in ferment and that Christian mission was on the eve of its greatest challenge and opportunity. Soon after he wrote the book Dr. Latourette was killed in an automobile accident. Were he alive today, he would still point with convincing finger to the time just ahead as the "tomorrow of tomorrows" already dawning for all of mankind and especially for Christians.

Some will say, "It's always been like that, and tomorrow is always the climax of yesterday"; and they are right. History has always moved toward a significant tomorrow, and that tomorrow is always dawning today. The significance of Dr. Latourette's prophesy is that he could speak from a vast knowledge of history and an intimate commitment to the Word of God. For him Ephesians 3 is reality: God has a plan for the ages and his plan centers in Jesus Christ. It is an unfolding plan that seeks the redemption of all people. It rests upon the church, and it moves toward triumphant victory.

"What's past is prologue," wrote Shakespeare in *The Tempest*. Latourette had a vast knowledge of that "prologue" of evil and sin. He could see the unfolding wrath of God against all wrong. He knew that mankind's last great hope is the manifestation of the gospel of Christ to all people, a bold mission to a lost world. Just as Jesus spoke tomorrow's truth in his day, and as Christians have always done, we must do too. Tomorrow is here and we must speak to it.

THE SITUATION OF THE EIGHTIES

But what is the tomorrow of history really like? What do we see now that tells us what problems lie ahead? Recently a special

37

planning committee of Southern Baptists conducted a study to answer these questions in light of the churches' responsibility for missions. It identified sixteen challenges and opportunities that press upon the churches.[1] These are problems that both describe the churches' special situation and point up their pressures. Following is an adaptation of that material.

1. Family Life—Dealing with problems of deteriorating marriages and changing families.

Three recent surveys of selected church leaders point to the family as the number one problem faced by the churches. This problem includes low view of the marriage commitment, rising permissiveness, confusion of male and female roles, and apathy of parents.

2. Mission Involvement—A rising interest in missions and Bold Mission Thrust.

Baptists devoutly believe that the gospel is for the whole world and that it is the answer for all mankind's moral, spiritual, and even political difficulties. Bold Mission Thrust is both the challenge and the answer. Preaching the gospel to every person on earth by the year 2000 is the task Baptists have set out to accomplish. It is our greatest challenge.

3. Leadership Development—Preparing and involving lay persons in discipleship and leadership.

In almost every survey made of Southern Baptist work this emerges as a problem of high priority. One of every ten church members must serve as a leader in some capacity if the church is to be effective in its work. This means that with 13,000,000 members Southern Baptists need 1,300,000 leaders.

4. Bible Learning—Taking advantage of the widespread interest in Bible study.

The last ten years has brought an unprecedented revival of interest in Bible study in Southern Baptist churches. Dedicated adults are engaged in serious searching of the Scriptures. Many are involved in home study programs. In Christian history periods of great advance have been preceded by intense study of God's Word. If this pattern repeats itself, the years ahead will bring unprecedented growth in the churches.

5. Church Fellowship—Preparing a caring fellowship that recog-

nizes and develops the need for personal relations between persons drawn to each other in Christ.

The churches have lately come to recognize (1) the power of fellowship for evangelism and (2) the power of the fellowship for personal Christian discipline. Once the Christian submits himself to it, the fellowship becomes a life force for his daily living. In response to this, church membership will become more meaningful and this will bring a more attracting evangelism.

6. Aggressive Evangelism—Witnessing to the unreached masses.

Listing this as a basic challenge and opportunity is out of a conviction that a church is wasting time unless it is making new Christians. Without aggressive evangelism, it is slowly going out of business. New methods and new concerns will open the way for God's spirit to move once again among his people.

7. Efficient Communications—Using modern technological means to communicate the gospel.

For fifty years wave after wave of radical social change has swept mankind. None has affected life more than the communications revolution. Yet the communications revolution is just beginning.

8. Urban Life—Reaching the great cities with the gospel of Christ.

One out of every six Americans lives within the corporation limits of a city of 500,000 or more. By the year 2000 it is likely that 60 percent of the United States population will live in four great metropolitan belts: the Atlantic Seaboard, the Lower Great Lakes, the California Region, and the Florida Peninsula.

9. Human Suffering—Motivating the denomination to help meet the world problems of human hunger and human rights.

Freedom and hunger continue to be two of the world's most pressing human problems. In many countries the people do not have the rights of suffrage, of property, of vocational choice, or the freedom to live where they wish. Jails are filled with political prisoners. The lack of food is also a major problem. Probably two-fifths of mankind is undernourished. Nearly two billion people in the developing countries are living at starvation levels with low vitality, high vulnerability to disease, and short life expectancy.

10. Personal Adjustment—Helping persons whose roles in life are changing to find personal fulfillment in their new condition.

Accelerated change of the social, economic, political, and physical environments puts extraordinary stress on the individual. Sometimes these changes lead to radical adjustment in life-style and life vocation. The churches must respond to this problem.

11. Influencing Community Life—Ministering to the communities' spiritual and moral needs.

Most authorities agree that the most significant shift in values during the last twenty years is the ascendency of individual rights over cultural rules. People seem to expect that anything they want to do is their right, even if it goes against community norms. This threatens our whole value system. If it is broken without swift and adequate replacement, the foundation of society will be destroyed.

12. Christian Morality—Influencing society with Christian moral values.

The special values of the Christian faith have long been the foundation of Western law and order. They are the basis of such social institutions as family, education, welfare, and even government. Without them the world would regress in morality thousands of years. More than ever enemies of Christ are criticizing his values. Such pressures create grave problems for the churches, but they also give them their greatest opportunities.

13. Positive Leadership—Meeting the waves of social, economic, and political crises that threaten the stability of society.

Alarmist leaders are not likely to save the nation from turmoil. Faced with crises such as economic fluctuations, energy shortages, social aberrations, political upheavals, the alarmist tends to magnify these to catastrophic proportion. Christians must realize that they are among the silent leaders of society. Ordained of God to be leaven in the meal of life, they must act with deliberate poise to keep things calm all about them.

14. Problem Solving—Reconciling the mammouth discontinuities and conflicts that exist in society.

Five pressures bear down upon all mankind: (1) scientific and technological revolution, (2) unexpected complexities of our world, (3) our behaviour toward other persons with whom we must relate on a global scale, (4) rapidly increasing population, and (5) diminishing natural resources. These create tension sometimes beyond the mind of man to grasp. They set up great disorienting discontinuities.

- The largest populations exist in lands of most limited resources.
- The oldest and most learned governments are not always the most dynamic.
- The resources of the world are not evenly distributed.
- The nations of the northern hemisphere command 80 percent of the world's wealth and trade, 90 percent of the industry and services, and nearly all the institutional research.
- The inventiveness of the human mind does not now appear to be solving some of the problems dependent on technical solutions.
- The people most free are not always the most efficient.

15. Cross-Culture Expansion—Establishing new congregations in ethnic and cross-culture communities.

America has always been a pluralistic nation but today it is more so than ever. The Home Mission Board does mission work among more than a dozen major language groups. Black and Spanish populations are growing much faster than white populations. Some leaders think that in a few years Texas and other Southwestern states will be bilingual. All of this imposes on the churches a new look at their mission obligations.

16. Women Power—Finding new and creative ways for women to serve.

No one can read the New Testament without realizing the important and responsible place women have in the churches. In today's world that has a heightened appreciation of womanhood, it is more than ever necessary for the churches to find creative ways to use their services, or better still to encourage the women themselves to find these new opportunities for ministry.

IMPLICATIONS FOR CHURCHES

This picture of the world situation faced by the churches may seem extreme to some, yet all evidence points to its reality. If it is true, what then will be the bearing on the churches? What generally will be the shape of the churches in the world to come? Following is a scenario for what might possibly happen.

1. The Life and Character of the Local Church

The future shape of the local church in America will be greatly influenced by the energy problem. If the crisis is as serious as some authorities say, the churches will be radically changed just as all of American life will be changed. If it is not extremely serious, there will be some change; but the churches will endure. There will be new challenges and new opportunities. Probably (1) there is an energy crisis; (2) it is not as disastrous as some think or as nonexistent as some think; and (3) the economic changes brought about by the energy crises will be determining factors as gasoline and other fuels needed for personal mobility grow increasingly scarce. This will profoundly affect the churches.

Karl Rahner once said that there will always be the "little flock," small groups of believers meeting here and there away from the places people throng. Is this a prophecy of retreat? Surely there will always be the little flock, but this is not necessarily retreat or defeat. Just as medieval cathedrals are relics of the past, the huge church plants of today could become outmoded and unusable, especially if energy supplies are greatly diminished. This possible but not inevitable extremity will not be defeat for Jesus Christ.

Though still institutional in character, the churches of tomorrow may be smaller and less tied to huge, energy-demanding buildings. Buildings will be less formal and will be designed to foster true koinonia. As the little flock becomes spiritually stronger, a new evangelism based on group solidarity will emerge. It will be much more effective than some of today's evangelism. The church will continue to worship as it does now except that the sermon may be more important, becoming increasingly instructive in nature. It may become the main channel for teaching the faithful. Preaching will be shared, with both ordained and unordained participating, women as well as men; but there will always be the pastor who will be the leader of the flock.

42

Churches may need to share buildings; and buildings may be used continuously especially on the days of worship, with groups attending at different hours. The churches will foster programs paid for by tithes and offerings, but there will be increased awareness of the need for personal ministry in locally fostered social action and mission action projects. As the churches grow in koinonia, the members will grow also in awareness of the need to minister to each other and to their neighbors.

Even the smallest church must be organized and administered. It must be promoted, and above all it must be led. Churches without strong leaders will fade away. The leaders must have a sense of mission and a feeling for organization. They must see these as spiritual tasks.

There appears now to be a diminishing emphasis on uniformity even in the largest and oldest and most tradition-bound denominations. It may be less and less possible to have a national uniform program of any kind. This does not mean there will be less organization, only less uniformity. Groups of similar conviction will coalesce. Their unity will likely be one of mission, not necessarily one of method.

If energy continues to be a serious problem, some churches will meet seasonably, especially those located in the harsher climates. Diminished energy will bring some blessings to the churches. With travel greatly reduced people may find they have more time for church. The church fellowship may again become the members' chief social opportunity. Families may become stronger. If this happens, the churches will greatly benefit.

2. The Use of Time and People in the Local Church

There is nothing biblical about the eleven o'clock hour except that it is on the Lord's Day. Many churches now are finding other more suitable hours for worship. For many, eleven o'clock may still be the most convenient time. If American churches were beginning anew, many perhaps would select it as the best hour for worship.

The important thing is the purpose of the gathering of the church. Why does it meet? What does it do at the gathering? If worship, evangelism, Bible study, and koinonia are important and necessary, then the church should gather as often as there is need for these. Churches that gather often seem to thrive, and those that do not seem to languish and die. In New Testament times the strongest churches appeared to meet daily. In today's time the strongest churches meet at least three times weekly. The future should bring no change in this, except that energy problems may mean some adjustment in the distance people drive to church and the number of times the churches meet.

As churches grow more numerous and closer to the homes of the people, the members will not necessarily become less active. Fifty years ago people were walking two or three miles to church two or three times weekly. Fifty years from now they could do the same if necessary.

The church must learn the Bible and it must evangelize. These go hand in hand. Whatever its location, the congregation must gather for these purposes. Other programs may diminish, yet these must live or there may not be the little flock anywhere.

3. The Place of Education in Tomorrow's Churches

One cannot read the New Testament without becoming aware of the role of teaching and study in the life of the church. The churches thrived on what they learned of the gospel. This tradition was continued among the early church fathers, and the progress made through the third century was largely due to the way in which the churches learned the fundamentals of Christianity.

The true churches of today are not any less well learned. The same will be true of tomorrow's churches. Compared with today there may be some differences. Preaching will become increasingly instructive and oratorical. As preachers see more the ruin of materialism, they will emphasize Christian values and will be fired with a new, desperate zeal. The Bible more than ever will be the central textbook of the churches. Bible classes will develop wherever people gather for work or for social activities. Unless there is a disastrous lack of energy, the Sunday Schools will continue to exist. In many areas, they will grow and will become more than ever the vital evangelistic arm of the churches.

In huge metropolitan areas where population is highly concentrated there will be an increase in "house" churches. Some will remain stationary for relatively long periods of time; others will be migratory, moving from house to house. These churches will be fluid in membership and doctrine. These house churches will flourish only as long as the economy prohibits them from owning their own buildings or at least partnership in buildings. To really grow, the churches will always need at least partnership in buildings. To really grow, the churches will always need at least semipermanent domiciles. These buildings will determine in some ways the nature of Christian education.

Parents are becoming concerned over the lack of true Christian education for children in some of the church schools. Following the lead of secular educators, some local leaders have substituted the impressionistic casual learning methods for traditional methods that emphasize biblical content. The absence of concrete biblical material is of great concern to many parents. This is likely to change as Christian educators sense the need for explicit biblical material. There will be increased use of the Bible in the instruction of the very young.

4. The Place of the Home in Spiritual Formation

For a great many people the home and the family are becoming more important than ever in the religious education of children and youth. Among older parents today there is widespread feeling that the churches have faltered in the teaching of Christian truth to children and youth. They have provided music education somewhat, social education and opportunity largely, but true religious education not enough. For sincere Christian parents this could mean less dependence on the Sunday School and other church programs and more on what they themselves do in the home. It possibly will not mean less involvement in church activities but more awareness of parental responsibility for teaching Christian knowledge and values.

As churches become aware of this, they will (1) create an even wider consciousness among parents of parental responsibility, (2) take steps to improve church educational programs, and (3) provide materials to help parents in the home do better work in the religious education of the young.

Somewhere sometime the pastoral ministry will become more consciously educative. The pastor will become as much an educator as preacher. He will teach and he will equip others to teach.

5. The Evangelism of Churches of Tomorrow

Truly if the church survives, it will do a better job in evangelism; but to do it there must be some changes. First, church members will have to become more highly disciplined. The Christian life must be seen as different from other lives. Congregations will be composed of some persons committed to full membership and other persons who are learners. Crossing the line into membership must be a real experience, not an empty signing up as it has been in the past.

Second, evangelism must find its power in the spiritual koinonia of the church. This is because the Spirit of God is most visible in the united life of the church. The strength of evangelism will be the strength of the group appeal of God's people. More stresses will be placed on coming under discipline of the group.

Third, more than ever the teaching of the Bible will become the open door of evangelism. Group Bible study will be one of the main evangelistic methods. It will not replace preaching, but it will become an important adjunct to preaching.

Fourth, personal witness of one individual to another will continue and possibly increase. As in the past it will be the first step toward drawing the lost into the group. As Christians learn the futility of harsh abrasive talk, and as they learn to conduct themselves wisely toward outsiders, making good use of time, letting their speech be gracious and seasoned with salt (cf. Col. 4:5-6), they will become more effective in evangelism. They will learn to talk effectively in convincing others of the gospel of Christ. More programs will be turned toward helping church members do this.

Fifth, preaching will become less oratorical and more instructive, less contrived and more filled with the Spirit. As preachers become more immersed in the harsh failures of today's humanity, they will revive preaching on the biblical doctrine of sin. This will lead to a new sense of urgency and earnestness.

There will be a new yearning in preaching, manifest not in shouting but in zeal, not in words but in communication. All this and more if God's Spirit is allowed absolute sway.

Radio and television evangelism will continue in importance. Yet if it is effective, it must have new credibility.

6. The Responsibility of the Laity in the Church

Ever since the publication of *Theology of the Laity* by Hendrick Kraemer, American Protestants have been talking a great deal about lay ministry and striving a little bit to put it into practice. So far, the movement has languished, perhaps succeeding here and there, but in the main outrightly failing. Church members generally are good neighbors. They serve their own congregational koinonia well, and they extend friendly hands to their neighbors; but in the main, they do not minister to the world. Even in the koinonia they seldom engage in preventative ministry, only in crisis ministry, and that not too fervently.

This may change, due partly to all the talk of the past two decades and partly to a new understanding of the pastor as equipper. If this happens, we can expect (1) a new appreciation of what it means to be a Christian in the world, (2) a reorientation of church programs toward people in distress in the community, (3) a new tenderness in the church, with members more conscious of one another's burdens and more inclined to bear one another's burdens, (4) an increased discipline in the church with more individuals more willing to submit to it, (5) better understanding by the laity of the role of the minister in the congregation, (6) a restatement of the image of the ministry with clear lines drawn between types of ministries, and (7) a wide acceptance of the bivocational minister. All of this will require special training. Denominational leaders will become equippers of the equippers. The pastors themselves will more than ever sense their roles as leaders and equippers in ministry.

---

1. Orrin Morris and Albert McClellan, *The Situation in the Churches—the 1980's*, a background paper for SBC and state convention program leaders, draft edition, January 1979.

47

Chapter 4

Priority Concerns in the Eighties

To what vital issues should the church be speaking during the decade of the eighties? This is always a dangerous question because needs and trends have a way of changing very quickly.

But three issues that Southern Baptists have chosen for emphasis during this decade give evidence of staying with us for a while. Churches that insist on ministering where the action is will have evangelism, family ministry, and Christian discipleship somewhere near the top of their list of priorities.

EVANGELISM

Evangelism is and will always be a priority concern of Southern Baptist churches. The commission of our Lord Jesus Christ commands it, the terrible destiny awaiting lost souls requires it, personal spiritual growth of saved persons depends upon it, and the advancement of the Kingdom of God waits for it.

Bold Mission Thrust, an emphasis launched by Southern Baptists, aims to give every person in the world the opportunity to hear and accept the gospel by the year A.D. 2000. Although supported by Southern Baptist Convention agencies, the success or failure of this project will depend upon the evangelistic emphasis and actions of local churches.

Demonstrating the love of Christ to every person in the community where a church assembles for worship is imperative. Sharing the good news of the gospel face-to-face with persons in every community is essential. Persons receiving Christ as Lord and Savior must be nurtured toward Christian maturity in the warm, compassionate atmosphere of a loving, evangelistic church. Each church should evaluate its expenditure of time, personnel, and money, and compare the amount spent for outreach with that spent on church members. More money and effort must be given to reaching the lost for Christ.

49

The first step a church must take is to recognize that it is God's will for it to be evangelistic. Then the leaders and members should make a commitment to grow an evangelistic church.

1. An Atmosphere of Prayer

A church is unlikely to become evangelistic unless the members experience spiritual awakening. This does not mean that every member will reach the same level of spiritual maturity. It does mean that the presence and the leadership of the Holy Spirit should be evident in the lives of church members in corporate worship services in the church.

Church historians have discovered that there has never been a spiritual awakening that did not begin with fervent, agonizing prayer. Unless the church commits itself to spiritual awakening, it will be impossible to become evangelistic in the true biblical sense. Prayer is the foundation upon which evangelistic churches are built.

2. Concern for All People

The spiritual condition of people who live in the vicinity of the church building must be determined. Although most churches attract members and visitors from some distance, every church has a responsibility to share the good news of Jesus Christ with those who live within a certain geographical proximity to the church building. To fail to share the gospel with persons nearby is to fail to take the Great Commission to the world for which God has made each church responsible.

A people search of a clearly defined geographical territory near the church building is imperative. The name, address, age, needs, and spiritual condition of every person in this area must be learned and recorded. This information should be continually updated.

A cultivated witnessing plan should be started by the church so that every unsaved person and unenlisted Christian will be shown a loving, caring concern by a committed Christian in the name of Jesus Christ. Making friends for Jesus Christ is one of the greatest privileges of Christian witnessing.

3. Systematic Plan of Bible Study

Various suggestions on how a church can enlist persons in the study of God's Word are given in chapter 7. The Holy Spirit uses God's Word to convict persons of sin. He also uses the written word to help Christians grow toward the likeness of Jesus Christ. An evangelistic church must use every means of enrolling people in Bible study to help them grow into spiritually mature Christians.

4. Organized for Evangelism

An evangelistic church makes maximum use of all church program organizations and committees to reach people for Christ. When the church is permeated with a commitment to reach people, each organization and committee can measure its success by how it contributes to this commitment.

Churches are organized differently to do evangelistic work. In some churches most evangelism is done by the pastor. But no pastor can do all the witnessing for a church. Pastors should consider themselves trainers or equippers of witnesses. A pastor can multiply his ministry best by training others to witness.

Sometimes deacons, the Sunday School, or the church council are assigned primary responsibility for evangelism in the church.

An excellent way to keep evangelism central in the church is to elect an evangelism committee. This committee will consult with and assist the pastor in developing the presenting to the church council or congregation an aggressive and perennial program of evangelism.

The chairman of the evangelism committee will be a member of the church council. The church council will support and assist in implementing evangelism goals and actions recommended by the evangelism committee and approved by the church. He should seek to permeate the church and its organizations with the spirit of evangelism. Churches which have an evangelism committee can use the members to assist the pastor in planning, implementing, and following through evangelism projects approved by the church. The duties of the evangelism committee are listed in chapter 11.

5. Equipping People to Witness

The greatest need of most churches is to enlist a corps of persons who can be equipped to witness effectively for Jesus Christ. They need to be equipped to witness when given a specific assignment. But they also need to be motivated to witness through the traffic patterns of their living. Motivation is the key to witnessing. When we love Jesus Christ and lost people, we will find a way to tell them about Christ.

Several excellent methods of equipping Christians to witness have been developed by Southern Baptists. Lay evangelism schools are a proven method of training persons to witness through a combination of classroom and exercises and on-the-job training.[1] TELL modular training also is an effective tool to train individuals and small groups to share Christ with others.[2] The Equipping Center Module on "How to Witness" is a method for specialized training in Christian witness.[3]

A continuing witness training process is being developed to enable the church with no training, some training, or much training to develop an effective program of training and multiplying Christian witnesses.[4] Already available is the training process and some materials which will enable the pastor to begin with himself and two trainees. He can start with a larger number if he has more persons in the church trained to witness, assigning one trainer for each two trainees. The continuing witness process will develop trainers who can enlist other trainees for the purpose of learning to witness.

6. Using Mass Evangelism

Mass evangelism, especially church revivals, simultaneous revivals, and area crusades, is an excellent method for reaching people with the gospel. If preceded by adequate preparation and proper follow-through, revivals and crusades are proven methods for reaching people for Jesus Christ.

Newspapers, direct mail, radio, and television offer churches a tremendous opportunity to create awareness of the need for salvation. Awareness of need must come before the conversion experience. Until the Holy Spirit convicts a person of sin, he cannot be saved. But churches shouldn't expect a media campaign alone to reach people for Christ. There is no substitute for person-to-person, face-to-face presentation of the good news that God sent his only son, Jesus, into the world to save sinners.

Mass evangelism events should be preceded by personal witnessing encounters between individuals. Mass evangelism events should be followed up by personal witnessing to persons who have indicated any decision for Jesus Christ.

FAMILY MINISTRY

Family ministry is a second priority concern of Southern Baptists in the eighties. To illustrate his relationship to his people, God used the analogy of the family. God is the Father; we are his children; the church is the bride of Christ. This picture makes it clear that the family is important to God.

After creating the first man and the first woman, God brought them together in a marriage union. Mutual needs of the man and woman and their potential for meeting these needs was God's plan. Then he charged them to "be fruitful and multiply" (Gen. 1:28). Soon, with the blessing and sanction of God, children were born into this home.

Throughout the books of Law God emphasized the responsibility of parents for the religious training of their children. Parents' relationship to God was to be a vital part of their everyday life in the home.

During his earthly ministry, Jesus showed his concern for the family. On one occasion he attended a wedding and blessed it by performing a miracle and by participating in the celebration. In his response to the Pharisees' question about divorce, he supported the teaching of the Old Testament about the sanctity of marriage and the family. And he added his own statement about God's ideal of permanence in marriage: "What therefore God hath joined together, let not man put asunder" (Matt. 19:6).

The apostle Paul had practical things to say about marriage and family relationships. In Ephesians, for example, he called upon members of a family to submit themselves "one to another in the fear of God" (Eph. 5:21). The relationship of Christ and the church becomes the model for relationships within the family (Eph. 5:24-25). Writing to Timothy, Paul even made caring for one's own family a test of orthodoxy: "But if any provide not for his own, and specially for those of his own house, he hath denied the faith, and is worse than an infidel" (1 Tim. 5:8).

1. Families Need Help

American families are falling apart by the thousands each year because they are unable to cope with their problems. A deep sense of urgency to help strengthen family life is being born out of this deep family trauma. Both the church and denominational leaders now feel a mandate from the Lord to provide ministries to help the family. The strength of the nation is dependent on the strength of its families. The strength of the church is dependent on the strength of its families.

The task of the family ministry program of a church is to minister to the distinctive needs of families, senior adults, and single adults.

Families within a church and community vary in size, age, needs, life-style, situation, and circumstances. Many families are composed of the traditional father, mother, and children. Others consist of single persons rearing children, or the divorced, widowed, or never married living in their own homes, often alone. Then there are those couples whose children are gone from home.

Many persons find happiness and satisfaction in their families. Others feel the need for affirmation, encouragement, and loving expressions. Some are grappling with great stress, physical, emotional, or spiritual. The church has a responsibility to minister to the needs of families at every stage of development.

2. Life Cycle Needs of Families

Unique adjustments are required at every stage of the family life cycle. Churches should be alert to these adjustment needs.

The premarital years are a time when young people need the church. They need premarital education in all areas of family life, but perhaps the greatest need relates to their concept of marriage. The expectations of many couples go no further than "living happy ever after." Engaged couples need premarital counseling, but long before engagement they need premarital education. Both their parents and their churches have an obligation to prepare couples for marriage.

Newly married couples, regardless of their ages, face many adjustments. Learning to live together, to manage their finances, to meet each other's needs, and deciding whether to have children—these are some of the concerns of newlyweds, whether they are young adults or in their senior years. Churches may be of significant help to couples at this stage of their marriage.

The parenting years have their distinctive needs. Parents need an understanding of growth needs of children and the meaning of discipline. The development of self-esteem in children is crucial. Many parents need training in how to cultivate self-esteem in their children. Bringing children up in the "nurture and admonition of the Lord" is a concern of Christian parents. They need help from their church in this important task. Children and youth need the help of the church in relating to their parents and in laying foundations for their future family life.

Parents in this age group are frequently caught between two generations. Many have responsibility for aging parents and must, in some cases, provide financial as well as emotional help while they also have responsibility for their own children. The need for marriage enrichment during the parenting years is significant.

The empty nest years bring on the need for preretirement training and preparation, although preretirement training will be most effective if begun earlier. Emotional preparation is as important as financial preparation for well-adjusted retirement, and neither can happen overnight. Many couples need help in letting their children go. Couples may also need help in strengthening their marriage relationships and adjusting to their primary roles as couples instead of parents. Women, especially, may feel useless at this time unless they have built good marriage relationships.

Retirement and adjustments in the later years of life often bring unique feelings of need. Retirees may feel useless. Their self-esteem may be low unless they are affirmed as persons of worth. They need to learn to use their new leisure time in meaningful ways. The church family can be of great support in opening new avenues of service for retired adults. Death is inevitable, but many people—even Christians—are not able to accept impending death. Churches have a responsibility to help people adopt realistic attitudes toward life and death.

3. Crisis Needs of Families

Opportunities for the church to strengthen and undergird families occur at every stage of family life. In addition, all families at one time or another face crises. Churches should support families during these times. Critical illness, death, divorce or separation, arrest of a family member, birth of a handicapped child, responsibility of an older family member, fire, tornado, flood, loss of job—these are some of the tragedies that bring on crises. Families are likely to need all kinds of help—from casseroles to sympathizing tears and hugs and promises of prayer support. Counseling by a professional is often needed. Along with the educational approach to family ministry, there will always be a need for crisis ministry.

4. Developing Family Ministry for Your Church

The first step in ministering to families is developing a sensitivity to the needs of families. The church must feel their hurts. It must have a nonthreatening, noncritical approach. "Neither do I condemn thee" must be the attitude of those who would help.

Programs or projects should be provided in the areas of priority concern. Priority concerns of families usually include marriage preparation education, marriage enrichment, family relationship development, parenting skills development, family crises ministry, mid-life and empty nest adjustments, preretirement planning, and adjustments to retirement and to the later years of life. The family ministry program of a church may be a variety of special projects designed and conducted to meet these specific priority needs. Ongoing activities may also be a part of the program.

CHRISTIAN DISCIPLESHIP

A third priority concern of Southern Baptists is Christian discipleship. The life of a church is dependent on the spiritual condition of its people. Growth in faith is at the root of all spiritual growth. This is necessary before church ministries and programs can come alive.

Growth in faith awakens our motives and desires and infuses our lives with spiritual energies. What is so often lacking in church and denominational programs is fervency and intensity of enthusiasm. Boldness for mission comes because of this intensity—being absorbed in it, caught up in it, wholly involved. Only discipleship, growth in faith, can bring that kind of spiritual fire to a church's life.

All Christians deserve the opportunity to grow in faith. Every new believer is expected to develop his or her full potential as a follower of Christ. Churches have a responsibility to provide this opportunity. These opportunities are made available through a church's training program that equips church members for discipleship. Equipping follows the growth process of the Christian from the time that person becomes a Christian, through learning the basic disciplines of the Christian faith, to developing spiritually qualified workers in the church. This process of discipleship development comes through new church member training, church member training, and church leader training.

A disciple is one who makes Christ the Lord of his life. Living the Christian life includes a disciplined study of Scripture, a daily experience with Christ, a nurturing and edifying relationship with other Christians through church membership, a vital prayer life, and an active witness to nonbelievers. Those equipped for discipleship will be making disciples—multiplying themselves through other believers.

This program of discipleship through church training includes the nurturing of new Christians, evangelism, doctrine, and leadership discovery and development.

1. Discipleship and Evangelism

Discipleship begins with evangelism. In evangelism we give witness to Jesus Christ and his work in our lives. Discipleship and evangelism are to be understood in the context of the Great Commission. The imperative of Matthew 28:19-20 to "make disciples" includes the entire process of winning persons to Christ and helping them grow in their Christian lives.

Discipleship and evangelism were inseparable in the ministry of Paul in the work of the early church. The book of Acts vividly describes how the early church practiced both. The church won many to faith in Christ and nurtured these converts in growth and faith (Acts 2:41-47). Paul clearly understood the work involved in making disciples. "They preached the good news in that city and won a large number of disciples. Then they returned to Lystra, Iconium and Antioch, strengthening the disciples and encouraging them to remain true to the faith" (Acts 14:21-22, NIV).[5]

Paul and Barnabas not only won many to Christ on their first missionary journey; they also nurtured the new believers and helped them to grow in their faith. In 1 Thessalonians Paul speaks of his intense evangelistic efforts in the city of Thessalonica (1 Thess. 1) and recounts his careful work in strengthening and equipping the believers (1 Thess. 2).

The local church is the primary agency through which equipping is to take place. The church is to be a fellowship through which members grow in loving relationships, mutual encouragements, and edification. In the church they should find motivation and spiritual energies for daily living.

New Testament churches were characterized by this dynamic witness to the world. The training and discipleship that churches offer will result in witnessing and outreach efforts to the world. With this ministry the church is built up and multiplies in numbers (Acts 9:31).

2. Discipleship and New Church Member Training

Evangelism will result in an expanding number of new Christians being added to the church. Like newborn babes, the new Christian has many needs. The objectives of new member training is to help this new Christian progress to the point where he or she is a fruitful, mature, and competent disciple. Through relationships to a new church family the new Christian experiences love, affection, and acceptance. This ministry to new believers comes through the work of the Holy Spirit as he warms our hearts in love, joy, patience, kindness, faithfulness, and self-control (Gal. 5:22-23).

New Christians need spiritual food. Their spiritual food is the Word of God. "Like newborn babies, crave spiritual milk, so that by it you may grow up in your salvation, now that you have tasted that the Lord is good" (1 Pet. 2:2-3, NIV).

A new Christian needs equipping. A growing believer needs to learn how to have a daily time of prayer and Bible study, how to memorize Scripture, how to do systematic doctrinal study, and how to share the gospel in a simple and clear manner. As new Christians learn the simple how-to's of the faith, they develop habits that will lead them to deeper involvement in the life and work of the church.

3. Discipleship and Doctrine

Doctrine provides the Christian with the categories of scriptural truth. Through the church training task of teaching doctrine, the believer is transformed through the renewal of the mind. Biblical doctrine is often the instrument through which persons are transformed through the work of the Holy Spirit. First Peter 1:23 says, "You have been born anew, not of perishable seed but of imperishable, through the living and abiding Word of God." (RSV)[6] Growth in faith is growth in understanding doctrinal truth. "You will know the truth" Jesus said, "and the truth will make you free" (John 8:32, RSV). Through the power of the Holy Spirit doctrinal truth can convey to us the mind of Christ. Growth in the Christian life involves an increasing ability to think biblically about our daily lives.

Unless we understand the great doctrines of the Bible, our Christian lives are resting on shaky foundations. We are prone to be tossed to-and-fro by every false wind of man-made ideas. All Christians are confronted day by day with many thoughts and pilosophies that can confuse and distort faith. Our study of the basic doctrines of the faith helps establish us in solid scriptural truth.

The Holy Spirit assists the Christian in applying sound doctrine. When we are able to apply doctrinal truth, we find ourselves growing in faith. "I have no greater joy than this," says John, "to hear of my children walking in the truth" (3 John 4, NASB).[7]

4. Discipleship and Leadership Training

The Holy Spirit equipped the leaders of the early church for service. Through the spiritual gifts given to these Christians, the Holy Spirit taught, guided, and empowered for witness, enabling those who led in nurturing, comforting, and assuring other Christians. Those persons in Acts who were growing in faith, "good men and full of the Holy Spirit," were gifted with spiritual power and wisdom for specific tasks of witness and ministry. The whole church in Acts received such an empowering for service (Acts 2:4; 4:31).

Spiritual gifts which edify the minds and hearts of others are given priority over those which nourish personal emotional experiences. The Christian who is equipped for service should always seek to please God. In that process we should expect God to give us the gifts we need to meet the particular needs that exist in the church. Romans 12:6-8 is an example of the gifts given for the church's life and witness—service, teaching, exhortation, giving, leading, and showing mercy.

Discipleship will lead persons into leadership roles. Each church should provide the kinds of training and the depth of training needed by those who are discovering their gifts for ministry. A church's training program should provide training needed by leaders in the church. A church's training program will cooperate with other programs in conducting specific job-related training. The general leadership of a church can be coordinated and conducted by using the resources available in the Church Training program.

A church on mission is dependent on a strong equipping and discipling ministry. When a church focuses on equipping the congregation, every Christian becomes a potential instrument of God to be used in the church's ministry. The cooperative efforts of the Church Training program with other programs and agencies will provide the denomination with the discipleship resources needed to equip the church for mission. Through these plans and resources both large and small churches may have a discipleship program that fits their needs.

1. Lay Evangelism School materials are available at Baptist Book Stores. Teachers for Lay Evangelism Schools can be secured through your state director of evangelism.

2. TELL equipment and leadership information is available through the Personal Evangelism Department, Home Mission Board, SBC, 1350 Spring Street, N.W., Atlanta, Georgia 30309.

3. Equipping Center Modules can be ordered from the Materials Services Department, Sunday School Board, 127 Ninth Avenue, North, Nashville, Tennessee 37234.

4. Information about Continuing Witness Training is available from your state director of evangelism.

5. From the New International Version New Testament. Copyright © 1972 by the New York Bible Society International. Used by permission of Zondervan Publishing House. Subsequent quotations are marked NIV.

6. From the Revised Standard Versions of the Bible, copyrighted 1946, 1952, © 1971, 1973 by the Division of Christian Education of the National Council of the Churches of Christ in the U.S.A., and used by permission. Subsequent quotations are marked RSV.

7. From the *New American Standard Bible*. Copyright © The Lockman Foundation, 1960, 1962, 1963, 1971, 1972, 1973, 1975. Used by permission.

Chapter 5

Mobilizing for Mission

A church that is effective is brought into being through prayer and conscious effort. It is oriented to the needs and opportunities of the community. It is established on solid continuing structures. Successful accomplishment of its mission becomes a matter of applying good principles and procedures of operation. Basic to the development of an effective church program is an understanding of how it should be structured.

The steel skeleton of a building has two functions: to hold the building up and to transfer the natural stresses created by its weight and design to other points where the stress is manageable. A church may be constructed in a similar way. The underlying structure is a group of programs with specific responsibilities and functions. The structure grows out of biblical foundations. It is based on understandings of what a church is, what it does, and how people work together as Christians. When a church is well founded and structured, it is able to meet the personal and spiritual needs of people.

The churches of the New Testament were organizations. In order to function, they appointed officers and leaders. They created structure and policies. They could not do their work without agreements about purposes and plans. System and order were important. All of these factors called for organization. But these churches were more than organizations. They had life. They were a part of the body of Christ. This made them unique organizations—unlike human institutions.

New Testament churches were self-governing under the lordship of Christ. They were autonomous congregations that managed their own affairs. While they cooperated with other churches, they were subject only to Christ. The church is like a democratic society in which all members participate and bear responsibility. In another sense, the church is a theocratic society; it exists under divine rule.

Southern Baptists have mounted a massive effort known as Bold Mission Thrust to reach every person on earth with the gospel by the year 2000. Such a challenge will call for a solid base of operation. It will require real growth of the churches and extra effort from the people who make up those churches. The good news is that the resources are available to meet the challenge.

A FELLOWSHIP EMPOWERED BY MISSION

The Holy Spirit directs and empowers the church for its mission. He also strengthens God's people for their constant fight with evil. The Holy Spirit provides needed resources for the conquest of Satan. He gives a spirit of power, love, and self-control. A church can do effective work for Christ only if it draws on the available power that the Spirit supplies.

Every church should seek for maximum moral and spiritual power in the lives of its members and in the body of the church as a whole. Powerless Christians and weak churches indicate the absence of the Holy Spirit. Jesus promised the power of the Spirit to his followers as they sought to accomplish their God-given mission. The coming of the Spirit released the church for its task and strengthened it for effective witnessing. The book of Acts repeatedly underscores this work of the Spirit in the life of the early church.

People of the congregation are more willing to become involved in the work of the church when they find their interests expressed in the plans and activities of the church. A statement of mission, plans, and actions, when developed by persons responsible for the work, point the individual and the church toward the same goals.

1. Clarify Intentions

A basic step in charting the direction of a church is the development of a church mission statement or statements. A missions statement describes the basic purpose for which a church exists and what it intends to accomplish. A mission statement can become the spring from which all church plans and activities flow. It will identify the reason for existence of a particular

64

church, as seen and understood by the people.

The experience of developing a statement of mission will help church members merge and refine their dreams and expectations. In working together on a statement of mission, persons and groups link their ideals and purpose so that all relate to the mission of the church.

It would be wrong to assume that the statement or statements of mission are simply the dreams and expectations of all the members added together. The statement does identify compatibility which provides the groundwork for leaders to use in planning, allocating resources, and conducting activities.

2. Lead the People to Develop a Statement of Mission

Two factors play a major role in the involvement of members in the life and work of a church. People are more willing to become involved when they find their interests expressed in the plans and activities. People tend to be more strongly involved when they have participated in the development of an idea or project. Encouraging church members to develop a mission statement is a good way to motivate them to do the work of the church.

The mission statement should be adopted by the church. The proposed statement should come from a long-range planning committee or the church council.

Here's one example of a church mission statement: "The mission of a church, composed of baptized believers who share a personal commitment to Jesus Christ as Savior and Lord, is to be a redemptive body in Christ, through the power of the Holy Spirit, growing toward Christian maturity through worship, proclamation and witness, nurture and education, and ministry to the whole world so God's purpose may be achieved."

A strong mission statement will contain an acknowledgement of the specific challenges, needs, and opportunities faced by that specific congregation.

3. Test Your Statement of Mission

Test the validity of your mission statement in the meaning it

65

conveys to the church members.

    (1) Does it create hope and faith?
    (2) Does it express the church's best value judgment?
    (3) Does it encompass the whole church?
    (4) Is it consistent with biblical teachings?
    (5) Is it stated in logical, consistent terms?
    (6) Does it speak to both needs and opportunities?
    (7) Can it be accomplished?

4. Involve All Organizations in Accomplishing the Mission

The capability of a church for accomplishing its stated mission will be increased if all church organizations are involved. If their involvement is artificial or peripheral, demotivation and isolation will likely occur. The church council can play an important role in getting all organizations involved in the work of the church.

A FELLOWSHIP ENRICHED BY FULFILLMENT

A church gathers to worship, to proclaim and witness, to nurture and educate, and to minister. These continuing actions may be called church functions.

1. Worship

Worship is encountering God in experiences that deepen a Christian's faith and strengthens his service. Worship may occur in public or in private.

2. Proclaim and Witness

In one of the first acts of his public ministry, Jesus called out followers who would share in his mission of preaching, calling for repentance and obedience to God. He taught them essential truths and sent them out to proclaim the kingdom of God and to witness to the compassion and power of the Father. Proclaiming God's work and witnessing to his grace is for all persons. This is the communication of the message of Christ. Its purpose is to bring all persons to confess Jesus as Lord and accept him as Savior.

3. Nurture and Educate

Nurture and education includes the whole process by which the church prepares persons for the acceptance of Christ and guides their development toward Christian maturity. This includes teaching, training, fellowship, and personal involvement. The nurturing function of a church helps individuals grow toward a mature Christian faith and life. It begins before conversion and extends throughout the Christian's life.

4. Minister

Jesus is the example of sacrificial, self-giving love. He went about doing good, ministering to human need, challenging abuses of power, instructing his followers to forget themselves and give themselves in gracious service to others. The ministry to which Christ calls his followers takes many forms. But its distinctiveness rests in the fact that it is done in his name and for his glory. Ministering is meeting crucial human needs in the spirit of Christ. It recognizes that a church must have concern for the whole person, the physical as well as the spiritual being. This includes the service a church and its members perform for the estranged, the destitute, the deprived, and the suffering within its own membership, in its community, and in the world.

A church will experience vitality of life, growth, and fulfillment through the functions of worship, proclamation and witness, nurture and education, and ministry as each Christian uses his gifts to serve God.

A FELLOWSHIP UNITED BY ORDER

A church needs a wide variety of ministries to respond to the many challenges presented by individuals and the community. Each person has a different set of needs that are as unique as his fingerprints. The church will find it impossible to minister to people in one way or through one or two programs.

Continuing activities of a church may be called tasks. Church tasks reflect the ways in which a church will pursue its mission. Task statements provide a clear definition of the continuing work of a church. Task statements, when grouped appropriately, provide an orderly division of a church's work. The grouping of tasks provides the basic structure for the church and allows programs to take initiative and assume responsibility for assigned areas.

Tasks should be consistent with a church's purpose and nature. Tasks for all church programs should be comprehensive of the total continuing work of a church. Task statements should be limited to one specific kind of church activity.

Church tasks are performed by three different types of programs in the church.

1. Basic Church Programs

There are six established church programs. Each of the six has a cluster of tasks that are basic, continuing, and of primary importance to the total work of a church. Each has significant organization and seeks to involve the total church in its work. These programs form the foundation of church structure. They are now referred to as basic programs.

Listed below are the tasks which have been grouped for assignment to each of these six programs:

Pastoral Ministries
(1) Lead the church in the accomplishment of its mission.
(2) Proclaim the gospel to believers and unbelievers.
(3) Care for the church's members and other persons in the community.
(4) Interpret and undergird the work of the church and the denomination.

Bible Teaching
(1) Reach persons for Bible study.
(2) Teach the Bible.
(3) Witness to persons about Christ and lead persons into church membership.
(4) Minister to Sunday School members and nonmembers.
(5) Lead members to worship.
(6) Interpret and undergird the work of the church and the denomination.

Church Training
(1) Equip church members for discipleship and personal ministry.

(2) Teach Christian theology and Baptist doctrine, Christian ethics, Christian history, and church polity and organization.

(3) Equip church leaders for service.

(4) Interpret and undergird the work of the church and the denomination.

Music Ministry

(1) Provide musical experiences in congregational services.

(2) Develop musical skills, attitudes, and understandings.

(3) Witness and minister through music.

(4) Interpret and undergird the work of the church and the denomination.

Brotherhood

(1) Engage in missions activities.

(2) Teach missions.

(3) Pray for and give to missions.

(4) Develop personal ministry.

(5) Interpret and undergird the work of the church and the denomination.

Woman's Missionary Union

(1) Teach missions.

(2) Engage in mission action and personal witnessing.

(3) Support missions.

(4) Interpret and undergird the work of the church and the denomination.

2. Service Programs

Three service programs encompass tasks that support the congregation and the six basic programs in doing their work. A service program has organization. It contains some characteristics similar to basic programs. These three service programs are media services, recreation services, and administrative services. Listed below are the tasks of each of these service programs.

Media Services.—Educate persons in the use of media and provide media and media services to support the church in the achievement of its mission.

Recreation Services.—Provide recreation methods, materials, services, and experiences that will enrich the lives of persons and support the total mission of the church.

Administrative Services.—Assist the church to plan its program, manage its resources, and govern its life and work.

3. Emphasis Programs

A third type of church program is an emphasis program. An emphasis program is a continuing concern or a cluster of continuing concerns of primary importance to a church in achieving its objective. An emphasis program is primarily interpreted and channeled by all appropriate church programs. It may or may not have organizational structure. Five emphasis programs have been identified: family ministry, stewardship, evangelism, establishing new churches, and vocational guidance. Listed below are the tasks assigned to these emphasis programs.

Family Ministry.—Minister to the distinctive needs of families, of senior adults, and of single adults.

Stewardship.—Develop Christian stewards and support Cooperative Program ministries.

Evangelism.—Develop and implement an effective strategy of evangelism which assists the church to aggressively evangelize the community.

Establishing New Churches.—Establish new churches.

Vocational Guidance.—Educate in Christian vocation and guide persons in church occupation and adjustment.

A church is a redeemed community created by God. It is the children of God called out and set in an estranged world to serve as salt, light, and leaven. It is a group of believers who share a common commitment to Jesus Christ. It is a Christian fellowship empowered by mission, enriched by fulfilling life and work, and united in total effort.

Chapter 6

Providing Leadership Through Pastoral Ministries

Pastoral ministries is a term that refers to guiding, protecting, feeding, and nourishing a church in order that the church may grow, develop, and reproduce itself in the world. Since churches are made up of persons, the ministry is to persons. Persons are served by organization, so the development and maintenance of organization that effectively meets the needs of persons is an important part of pastoral ministries. Pastoral ministries in a church is implemented primarily through the pastor, staff, deacons, and church council.

The program of pastoral ministries was demonstrated by Jesus as he trained the disciples for leading his called out people. Jesus was pastor to the disciples, proclaiming the truth about himself and helping them to better understand themselves and to become what they were capable of becoming. He challenged them through example and instruction to minister to persons. He cared for them in their disappointments and their victories. He encouraged them to live and work together as brothers, supporting and enriching each other. The result of his pastoral ministry was a group of apostles who were equipped to minister to the Jerusalem church as Jesus had ministered to them.

The book of Acts records the progress of the apostles and their successors in providing pastoral ministry in the churches that sprang up during New Testament days. Acts 6 illustrates the commitment of the apostles to proclaiming the gospel, guiding the church to make an organized response to the needs they discovered, and caring for the people who had become the church. Their pastoral ministry was blessed and the church continued to grow. The ordained laymen who joined with the apostles in ministering to the church and proclaiming the truth about Jesus made an important contribution to the church's growth.

The pattern of pastoral ministries which was introduced by Jesus and continued by the apostles has served churches well whenever it has been followed. But the book *Called to Joy: a Design for Pastoral Ministries* points out that this pattern has not always been observed in the church. Beginning with the fifth century and following through the Middle Ages, the congregational services of the predominant Roman Catholic Church consisted mostly of observing the sacraments. Little attention was given to preaching or to the pastoral care of people. The sixteenth century Reformation, plus the influence of the Anabaptists of this period, called church leaders and congregations back to a New Testament concept of ministry.

Throughout most of church history congregational life was simple. Pastoral ministry was expressed primarily through preaching, administering the ordinances, and caring for people in their needs. But all this changed with the development of a variety of organizations in churches. Church structure was influenced by the changes in the business world. The work and the relations of church leaders began to change. Pastors became leaders of churches with complex organization. Many of these churches expected pastors to make the church successful. Church success was viewed in the same way the business world viewed success—increase in membership and property value, and increase in cash flow with a good cash balance at the end of the year.

Since the mid-twentieth century Southern Baptist churches have given much attention to reexamining their objectives and finding appropriate ways to accomplish their objectives. The responsibilities of pastors, other staff ministers, and deacons have received serious study. Ephesians 4 has become the scriptural foundation for most expositions on pastoral ministry with the focal point being the "equipment of the saints for the work of ministry" (Eph. 4:12, RSV).[1]

THE WORK OF THE PROGRAM OF PASTORAL MINISTRIES

The influences that shape pastoral ministries in the eighties are biblical instructions and patterns, lessons from historical developments, and the needs of persons who live in the eighties. Effective pastoral ministries will grow out of what it means to be the people of God in our time and place. Churches that are faithful to the Great Commission of Matthew 28:19-20 will hold on faithfully to Jesus Christ while taking his message into an everchanging environment. Pastoral ministries has the challenge of enabling churches to keep the unchanging message of Christ's salvation alive and dynamic in a world that is pulsating with change.

1. Ministering to a Personal Church

Individuals have different personalities. No two personalities are alike, nor do they need to be. Personalities change as personal and environmental conditions affect them. Sometimes the changes are intentional. They come to a person when he processes information about himself and sets some personal growth goals. At other times the changes are reactionary. Personality reactions may be constructive, with growth as the result; but they are often negative and show up as defensive, retrenching, and hostile behavior. As individuals become aware of their personalities, they can determine the ways they want to change and the ways they want to remain the same.

One pastor became involved with a six-year-old child who caused him some concern. The pastor noticed the child's somber personality, his hesitancy to play and laugh like other first graders. When he visited his family and found a no-frills, no fun, work-ethic environment, he realized that the child had reason to believe that his behavior was normal while that of his classmates was abnormal. This child needed to be exposed to some alternative models of personality in order to develop his celebrative self.

Churches, like individuals, have personalities. Church personalities are different from each other, and one church's personality is not the same at all times. This is as it should be. Pastoral ministries is concerned with helping churches develop attractive, positive, winsome, and confident personalities. A church that is despondent and lethargic can become determined and confident, joyous, and purposeful if it is stimulated properly. Through preaching and teaching a church discovers the biblical way to hope and joy. Grace becomes more evident than guilt.

As pastoral ministries leaders provide leadership for the church, a sense of direction and a way to achieve can be revealed. Pessimism is replaced with growing optimism; loser personalities become winners. Pastoral ministries leaders reach out to touch the church, and care and loneliness are replaced with togetherness. A church that had crossed arms and closed hands opens its arms to the world and beckons with its hands for others to come to it. The cared-for become carers and cold fear is replaced with warm fellowship.

Pastoral ministries shapes church personalities. Leadership that is positive and purposeful stimulates confidence and enthusiasm. Leaders who have a healthy image of themselves and of other persons enable churches to develop healthy feelings toward themselves and others. Openness and trust expressed by church leaders generates warmth in a church. Church personality development is a vital responsibility for pastoral ministries leaders.

2. Ministering to an Organized Church

Paul introduced the analogy of the church as a body (1 Cor. 12:12-27). This symbol calls attention to the variety of needs in the body and the variety of gifts which the body possesses to minister to these needs. The healthy body is organized and functioning with each part making its contribution to the whole body and experiencing the life of the body in return.

Church life is body life. A church has many needs, but it also has people to meet all these needs. As the people are led to discover the needs to which the church should respond, they can also be led to discover and develop the resources they need to meet these needs. Church organization is the relationship of persons to persons and persons to tasks in ways that meet needs and help persons grow. Pastoral ministries cares for the church's body as it helps to develop and maintain healthy organization.

Through leading the church to study its needs and the needs of the world to which the church is commissioned, pastoral ministries helps the church develop the organization which responds to these needs. When a church discovers its mission in the world, it is ready to decide how to organize itself, how to group people and

74

assign responsibilities, how to accomplish its purpose.

Pastoral ministries leads the church to identify the needed organization, create the organization, support the organization with resources, and celebrate the contribution the organization makes to the life of the body. When effective leadership is provided, the body grows healthily. Each part (persons or organizations) of the body knows how it relates to the other parts. Each part supports the other parts and celebrates every accomplishment of all of the parts that make up the body. Pastoral ministries succeeds when "the whole body, being fitted and held together by that which every joint supplies, according to the proper working of each individual part, causes the growth of the body for the building up of itself in love" (Eph. 4:16, NASB).[2]

3. Ministering to a Powerful Church

Churches have been promised all the power they need to do the work of Christ effectively. Before commissioning the disciples to go into all the world with the gospel and make disciples, Christ told them that he had all power in heaven and earth. He made that power available to the disciples so they could live out his life in the world. He makes it available to churches today for the same purpose.

Pastoral ministries has the responsibility to help the church know that this power is available, to help it claim the power through faithfulness to the nature and mission of Christ, and to use the power to the glory of God. As the gospel is preached and hymns of the faith are sung, as people are led in Bible study and prayer, as the people grow in willingness to be like Christ in the world, their power and their influence on the world multiplies. Pastoral ministries leaders call the people to open their lives to the presence of Christ so they may experience his power in them and in the church.

Christ's power is given to a church for a purpose. Pastoral ministries leaders help the church to channel the power into actions that accomplish the church's mission in the world. Just as Simon was denied the power that was evident in Peter and John because his motives were wrong (Acts 8:18-20), churches are denied the power of the Spirit of God when they want to use the

75

power for selfish or unworthy purposes. Pastoral ministries leaders have the responsibility to help the church focus its attention on the will and way of Christ so the power available to them will be used constructively.

4. Ministering to a Frontier Church

Churches that are faithful to their mission are always living a frontier life. Pastoral ministries leaders serve as explorers and guides for a frontier church. They help the church explore new worlds of need within the church and beyond it. They guide the church in settling the frontier land for growth and fruitfulness. The frontier spirit is characteristic of churches that keep looking for additional people to serve with the gospel as well as additional ways to serve people. The frontier spirit may cause a church to reorganize its ministry in order to experience new life. It may cause a church to begin a ministry to persons it has not served before in its community. The frontier may be in another part of the world or on another continent, but it can be explored and developed as the church is led to a bold mission venture.

Pastoral ministries leaders, by their calling and their gifts, are to go ahead of the church in study and exploration of the frontier life the church should live. They are then to go with the church as faithful guides to help it develop and implement programs of ministry that discover and develop the frontier. This is how pastoral ministries leaders help churches carry out the commission to go into all the world.

THE PEOPLE IN PASTORAL MINISTRIES

If churches on mission in the eighties are to be effective in ministry to their world, they need the help of capable pastors and deacons. Those churches that are complex either because of the size of the membership and the number of organizational units, or because of the diversity of ministries they become involved in, may need other staff ministers in addition to the pastor to help the church get its work done. Regardless of the size of the church, the pastor needs a staff of dedicated and trained volunteer workers to give leadership to the organizations through which the church does its work. These volunteers serve together as a church council. They are led by the pastor to serve the church through planning, coordinating, and evaluating the organizational activities a church on mission requires.

1. The Pastor Leads the Pastoral Ministries Team

Called to Joy: a Design for Pastoral Ministries places responsibility for pastoral ministries squarely on the shoulders of the pastor. "The pastor serves as leader of the pastoral ministries team. He is to lead the church in the accomplishment of its mission. The pastor is the leader of the entire church—all of its activities. He may function effectively or ineffectively, but he cannot escape the responsibility."[3]

Principles affecting church growth were thoroughly documented in research during the decade of the seventies. A principle that showed up consistently is that growing churches require pastors who are committed to helping churches grow, who believe that growth is possible, and who are willing to pay the price to be effective leaders. Pastors who give positive, joyous, faithful leadership to the congregation help to develop those qualities in deacons, other staff ministers, organizational leaders, and the entire church. This leadership is provided through preaching, teaching, guiding the church council and other organizational units and leaders, and through counseling with persons and groups in the church.

2. Deacons Serve with the Pastor in Pastoral Ministries

The biblical model for pastor-deacon relationships in pastoral ministries is found in Acts 6. While the seven who were chosen by the Jerusalem congregation for ministry were not called deacons, their ministry assignment and ministry style set the pattern for those who later came to be known as deacons.

The deacons' ministry assignment was to assist the apostles in serving the church by giving attention to the needs of the membership. They were asked to find the causes of murmuring and solve the problem so the fellowship could be restored and maintained. This would enable the apostles to continue giving their primary emphasis to studying the message of Jesus, praying, and preaching. The ministry of the deacons was no less spiritual or important than that of the apostles.

As deacons work with pastors, they minister to persons through loving, personal attention. The result is that persons who receive such Christlike attention are ready to listen responsively to the pastor and be guided by his preaching and his counsel. Even when a church does not have a pastor, deacons may effectively provide leadership, proclaim the gospel, and care for persons in the church and community.

Deacons may enlist yokefellows to work with them in ministering to persons. Yokefellows are not elected by the church. They are selected for a period of ministry along side the deacons.

3. Staff Ministers Serve in Pastoral Ministries

Many churches employ staff ministers who provide leadership as they are assigned responsibilities in pastoral ministries. "They assist with planning, conducting, and evaluating activities that relate to their areas of responsibility. This includes such leaders as associate or assistant pastor, minister of education, minister of music, minister of recreation, age group directors. It may also refer to volunteer workers who are elected to do the work often associated with employed leaders, such as volunteer music director."[4]

Staff ministers serve under the leadership of the pastor, but their calling and their role in ministry are not secondary to that of the pastor. Each has been chosen by God for a specific place in ministry that utilizes his personal gifts effectively. Each is involved in spiritual ministry that enables the church to carry out its mission in the world. The pastor is leader of the staff team because his role in the church and his accountability to the church are more comprehensive.

THE TASKS IN PASTORAL MINISTRIES

Pastoral ministries has four tasks that are ongoing in the life of a church: (1) lead the church in the accomplishment of its mission; (2) proclaim the gospel to believers and unbelievers; (3) care for the church's members and other persons in the community; and (4) interpret and undergird the work of the church and the denomination. Each of these tasks grows out of the instructions in Ephesians 4 to equip the saints for the work of the ministry. These tasks relate to the mission of the church to make disciples and to grow disciples in being and doing according to the life and teachings of Jesus.

Task 1: Lead the Church in the Accomplishment of Its Mission

A church assigns to pastoral ministries the leadership role in getting basic church tasks performed. This leadership involves helping the church determine the programs it needs and helping the church conduct its programs. As the need for professional leadership increases, a church may employ persons who will provide leadership in specialized programs of the church, such as education, music, recreation, outreach, or age-group ministries.

The focus of the leadership task is on persons. Organizations exist to meet the needs of persons. Pastoral ministries should approach this leadership role with primary concern for persons and personal relationships. This means leading the church to recognize the role of each member and to provide for relationships and activities that produce the greatest benefits for the church as well as individuals. The accomplishment of this task requires the best use of administrative skills.

Pastoral ministries leads the church to provide for planning, conducting, and evaluating its activities. This is accomplished as the church conducts effective business meetings and provides for a functioning church council and organizational councils. Officers and committees of the church plan, conduct, and evaluate assigned areas of work. The church should be led to plan for the future through short-range and long-range planning.

Pastoral ministries leads the church to discover and secure the proper relationship of persons to tasks. The church should be led to conduct a talent survey of the church membership. Pastoral ministries should work to create a climate in which workers may be enlisted and trained. As deacons visit regularly with church families, they can discover prospective workers and report them to the appropriate persons.

Pastoral ministries provides for adequate communication with church members. Effective communication is essential to successful administration. Church staff meetings and councils provide opportunities for effective communications. The church paper, bulletins, inserts, bulletin boards, letters, as well as direct visual and verbal contact in congregational services, are avenues along which effective communication may flow. Numerous personal contacts by the pastoral ministries leaders provide opportunities for interpreting the actions of church leaders and other church members. Pastoral ministries should assist in establishing means of communication and in keeping all channels clear.

Pastoral ministries inspires responsible participation in the work of the church. In personal ways—letters, home visits, phone calls—and in public expressions that are seen in print or heard in public gatherings, pastoral ministries encourages the commitment of fellow church members. Wise leaders are generous in commendation which is deserved and are careful to form a constructive relationship with those whose performance does not yet merit commendation.

Task 2: Proclaim the Gospel to Believers and Unbelievers

Pastoral ministries is responsible for leading the church in proclaiming the good news about Jesus Christ so persons will respond to him. Those who lead are expected to develop skills to achieve maximum effectiveness as proclaimers. They seek to lead all church members to become proclaimers to the extent of their ability and opportunity. They seek to discover and use all possible avenues in communicating the gospel.

The gospel may be proclaimed through public presentations, private conversations, written communications. The presentation of the gospel before an assembly of persons or by means of media such as radio or television is public proclamation. The Bible affirms preaching as the primary approach in public proclamation. Other approaches include teaching Bible truths, observing the ordinances, presenting the gospel in music, sharing personal testimonies, reading the Scriptures, and presenting religious drama and films.

Pastoral ministries assists church organizations in proclaiming activities, such as worship experiences in Vacation Bible School and at special camps and retreats.

In addition to these, proclamation activities may be conducted in special meetings away from the church. Churches may proclaim the gospel by conducting noon-day meetings in theater buildings and other places in the business center of the city. Opportunities may be found to proclaim the gospel publicly in places where groups normally assemble. Music and drama can be presented at shopping centers and other gathering places.

Church missions and chapels need the leadership of persons who can present the gospel effectively. Bold Mission Thrust highlights the need for more preaching stations.

There are more needs for proclamation in every community than pastors or other professional church leaders can meet. Their training and experience should qualify them to be the most able proclaimers, but circumstances do not permit them to proclaim everywhere. Deacons should be trained to work with the pastor in the task of proclamation. As these men serve effectively, they will inspire and enable others to join the ranks of those who proclaim through public presentations.

The gospel may be proclaimed in private conversation as efforts are made to lead persons to faith in Jesus Christ. The gospel is proclaimed in counseling as persons are led to grow in the application of the gospel to specific problems in their lives.

Deacons have an opportunity for proclamation through personal witnessing. The Deacon Family Ministry Plan offers a good approach for accomplishing this kind of ministry to families.

The gospel may be proclaimed in written communication. Daily newspapers may be used to present the gospel. A series of articles on fundamentals of our faith may proclaim to people who don't attend church as well as those who are members.

Tracts which present the gospel offer opportunities for proclamation. Pastoral ministries should lead the church to train persons in the effective use of tracts.

Letter writing is another way to proclaim the gospel. Personal letters reach persons who cannot be visited. These letters support and enforce personal witnessing.
not be visited. These letters support and enforce personal witnessing.

In addition to using daily newspaper, tracts, and personal letters, pastoral ministries should discover and develop the proclamation potential in brochures, flyers, bulletins, and church newspapers.

Task 3: Care for the Church's Members and Other Persons in the Community

A church is at its best when it is known as a community of believers who express the love of Christ to persons in need. All church members should be involved in individual and group expressions of concern. But some needs call for the skills of the leaders in pastoral ministries. These are needs that require professional attention because of their complex or delicate nature. Pastoral ministries leaders use their skills in responding to the critical needs of persons. They lead the church in organizing its resources and making them available for meeting this variety of human needs.

A church recognizes that people have many needs—spiritual, physical, mental, emotional, social—that call for help from persons who care. Leadership in this task requires specific actions on the part of pastoral ministries. Pastoral ministries helps church members become aware of the many needs of others.

Congregational services can help persons develop a healthy regard and honest awareness of others. Persons attending congregational services may be encouraged to speak with those around them and express their interest in them. Some churches use part of their midweek services to share concern for persons with specific needs which call for caring actions.

Pastoral ministries guides the church in developing and organizing its resources to help persons. A church can extend its caring ministry by maintaining a cooperative relationship with community agencies and cooperative ministries with other churches.

Pastoral ministries should involve concerned persons in ministering to others. As pastoral ministries leaders counsel with individuals and small groups, needs are discovered that can best be met by others in the church. Where there are persons in the church membership who have particular skills that are needed to meet particular problems, their help should be enlisted. Brotherhood and WMU may be a resource through their mission action work. Through the Deacon Family Ministry Plan deacons and their mates may provide caring ministry to all church families as they respond to the crisis and developmental needs of others.

82

Referral may be made to appropriate persons and agencies in the community whose resources are needed to bring help to individuals. Pastoral ministries leaders should know the available resources in the community and keep the channels of communication open. This cooperation in the community further challenges pastoral ministries to lead the church to become creative in the use of its properties to meet personal and community needs.

Task 4: Interpret and Undergird the Work of the Church and the Denomination

Pastoral ministries leaders succeed when the church succeeds. Good preaching or competent counseling alone will not build a church. Part of the success of pastoral ministries depends on interpreting and undergirding the work of the entire church.

The work of the church and the denomination may be interpreted and undergirded through preaching. Sermons that enable church members to grow will include support for church and denominational ministries and support for the work of the organizations as well as the entire congregation. Congregational services provide an excellent setting for supporting the work of the church and the denomination. Worship bulletins can carry important messages. Promotional and interpretation information may be presented as interesting and compelling announcements. Special prayer activities and congregational service features may undergird church and denominational emphases like stewardship promotion and Bold Mission Thrust.

Church newsletters or papers may carry attractive, timely articles about church and denominational life. Church council meetings may be used to channel church and denominational material through all church organizations.

Deacons, through the Deacon Family Ministry Plan, have many opportunities to talk with church members about the church and denomination. They can build goodwill and support as they channel information to their fellow church members.

1. From the Revised Standard Version of the Bible, copyrighted 1946, 1952, 1971, 1973.
2. From the *New American Standard Bible*. © The Lockman Foundation, 1960, 1962, 1963, 1971, 1972, 1973, 1975. Used by permission.
3. Ernest E. Mosley, *Called to Joy: a Design for Pastoral Ministries* (Nashville: Convention Press, 1973), p. 26.
4. Ibid., pp. 26-27.

Chapter 7

Reaching and Teaching with God's Word

God's Word, the Bible, is central to the work of Southern Baptists. The teaching of the Bible has been and continues to be the focus in Southern Baptist congregations. Thus, the Sunday School for the past seventy-five years has enjoyed a unique position in the work of the church. Through Sunday School many people have been brought into Bible study, and through this Bible study into a saving knowledge of Christ as Savior.

Why is the Sunday School so important to Southern Baptists? The purpose of this chapter is to answer this question. It will be answered in the context of the total church on mission. It will be answered with a recognition and appreciation for the other program organizations, support groups, and ministries which make up the total ministry of the church. It will be our purpose to see the Sunday School in this context, and at the same time to help church members rediscover the importance of the Sunday School.

What then is the Sunday School? What is the unique role it plays in the church?

SUNDAY SCHOOL IS THE CHURCH FULFILLING ITS MISSION

The mission of the church is to accomplish Christ's mission in the world. Indeed, the body of Christ—the church—is the people of God actively carrying out this mission.

Three passages of Scripture point us to this central purpose. In John 20:21 Jesus speaks to his disciples following the resurrection. On this occasion he tells them of his mission: "Peace *be* unto you: as *my* Father hath sent me, even so send I you."

A short while later the Greater Commission is given to the followers of Jesus. "Go ye therefore, and teach all nations, baptizing them in the name of the Father, and of the Son, and of the Holy Ghost: Teaching them to observe all things whatsoever I have commanded you: and, lo, I am with you alway, *even* unto the end of the world'' (Matt. 28:19-20).

Closely associated with this commission is the admonition of Christ in Acts 1:8: "But ye shall receive power, after that the Holy Ghost is come upon you: and ye shall be witnesses unto me both in Jerusalem, and in all Judea, and in Samaria, and unto the uttermost part of the earth."

Each of these passages points us to the clear mission of the church. In the eighties the church still seeks to accomplish its purpose. The means for actually putting this mission into practice is through the Sunday School. It is the responsibility of the Sunday School to teach the Bible. Through this Bible teaching, men and women, boys and girls are brought to Christ. Bible teaching is important in every Southern Baptist church. It must always be the focal point. It is proclaimed from our pulpits and shared through Sunday School classes and departments by Bible teachers. Why is the Bible so important to us? W. L. Howse and W. O. Thomason in their book *A Dynamic Church* clearly answer this question.

"The Bible provides the message to be shared. The message to be shared involves a person, an action, and a proclamation. The person of Jesus Christ is central in the message. The action, what God did in Christ for man, is the gospel—the good news. Paul described it in these words: 'I delivered unto you first of all that which I also received, how that Christ died for our sins according to the scriptures; and that he was buried, and that he rose again the third day according to the scriptures' (2 Cor. 15:3-4). Proclamation and witness are the Christian's part in carrying out the redemptive purpose of God. This is the only incomplete action in the story of redemption. All is now ready for lost man's response.

"In the Bible God reveals the means of spreading the good news. The means God prescribes for proclaiming the gospel is really simple: tell it and *live* it. The method is verbal—the story must be told. The setting for the story is the life of the messenger. The message must also be lived, and it must be lived in the world.

"At this point two commands to Christians may seem to contradict each other. One says 'be separate' and another says 'go into the world.' Both of these commands are binding. We can never fulfill our evangelistic mission in isolation. There is a delicate balance to be maintained. We must not separate ourselves from the people to whom the message is to be proclaimed.

"A redeemed humanity is in the mind of God. God created the world, and man is his highest creation. Man was made a living soul with mind and will. Man sinned and broke fellowship with God. From the beginning of the separation, God has continually sought man's redemption. The Bible reveals God's plan to redeem his lost creation.

"Would a church know the mind of God? Would God's people let his plan guide their lives? Then teach the Bible. Therein is revealed the mind and the will of God. Here is the open door for the leadership of his Holy Spirit.

"Christ expects his church to teach. The familiar commission given to the church culminates in teaching which leads to fulfilling the work of Christ. Jesus called his followers disciples. Disciples are learners, and learning is an educational experience. Disciples are to be taught to observe all that Jesus commanded about worshiping God, witnessing to men, learning the Christian faith, ministering to the needs of persons, and applying the Christian faith in every aspect of daily life. Here is something of the gigantic work a church is to do.

"The major issues confronting the world today are a concern to the Christian in his total assignment. They are significant for one who would follow Christ. From time to time, certain aspects of life come to the surface, demanding immediate and urgent attention. This is obvious in many of the great social issues of the day. Application in daily life is the natural expression of genuine Christian experience. James wrote: 'But someone will say, *"One person has faith, another has actions."* My answer is, *"Show me how anyone can have faith without actions; I will show you my faith by my actions"* (Jas. 2:18, GNB).

"Paul understood the place of teaching in a New Testament church. In Ephesians 4 Paul spoke of the various calls and assignments of Christ. Some are to be apostles; some, prophets;

some, evangelists; some, pastors and teachers. The educational approach is clearly identified. Teaching shares with other work in the full ministry of the Word and in the purpose of the churches. Paul described the educational assignment when he spoke of 'the perfecting of the saints, for the work of the ministry, for the edifying of the body of Christ: till we all come in the unity of the faith, and of the knowledge of the Son of God, unto a perfect man, unto the measure of the stature of the fulness of Christ' (Eph. 4:12-13). Leading men into a clear understanding of the revelation of God in the Bible must be a priority concern in the churches.''[1]

After understanding the importance of the Bible as central in the mission of the church, the next question is, How can this Bible truth be shared? Of course the obvious answer is by the people of God sharing the good news through Bible teaching. This is where the Sunday School takes its place in the mission of the church. The mission is accomplished by God's people organizing themselves in such a way as to discover people, involve them in Bible study, and seek to win them to Christ. The Sunday School is a means of accomplishing this mission.

The blending of a Sunday School program into the total work of the church—preaching, ministry, training, music—is truly the church fulfilling its mission.

SUNDAY SCHOOL IS ACCOMPLISHING THE TASKS OF THE CHURCH

It is important for any person seeking understanding of the church on mission to see how each part of the church fits together. It is additionally important for Sunday School leaders to understand the scope of Sunday School work. For this reason, each program has defined the tasks which are to be performed. This assures that no part of the church's mission is overlooked or duplicated by another program.

In order to understand what Sunday School work is, we need to become familiar with these six important tasks.

Task 1: Reach People for Bible Study

The purpose of this task is to involve as many persons as possible in Bible study. Reaching people for Bible study is a means of reaching people for broader involvement in the church. This reaching task is based on the assumption that Bible study will be used by the Holy Spirit as a foundation for drawing persons to Christ for salvation. Then they can grow in their commitment to live the gospel.

When applied, this reaching task means every member of the Sunday School who is a believer must be about the business of enlisting and involving in Bible study unsaved persons, unchurched Christians, members of a church who are not a part of the Bible teaching program, and children of those listed above.

The future Sunday School is mobilized to visit, to enroll others, and to cultivate and minister in the name of Christ. This means providing as many settings as possible to teach the Bible.

Task 2: Teach the Bible

The purpose of this task is to involve persons in the study of God's written revelation and in the application of its meaning to all of life.

The Bible is taught with the hope that persons may, under the leadership of the Holy Spirit, be led to respond to God with maturing faith, love, and obedience. This task assumes that teaching the Bible goes beyond learning facts and information. It involves understanding the message of God and its application to life.

Both Christians and non-Christians are taught the Bible together in the same setting in an ongoing plan of Bible study. The vast majority of these teaching experiences are conducted on Sunday morning in the church buildings. But in recent years other approaches outside the church building have been used to teach the Bible.

There are exceptions to ongoing plans of Bible study as well. Vacation Bible School and January Bible Study would be examples of those short-term Bible study experiences.

Task 3: Witness to Persons About Christ and Lead Persons into Church Membership

The purpose of this task is to discover persons who are not Christians among the Sunday School members and prospects and witness to them, and seek to lead them to Christ and to become members of the church.

Obviously this witnessing task is closely related to the first task of reaching people. In order to share one's witness through the Sunday School, a Christian must first discover the unsaved person, and, in many cases, involve him in Bible study.

The focus of this task, however, is in the follow-through of faith sharing. The Sunday School is incomplete in its total work until the Christian has shared his faith with those who do not believe in Christ as Savior. The witnessing task is not optional for Christians. It is at the very heart of the commission of our Lord. The Sunday School must be at the heart of that commission.

This task means that every Christian Sunday School member should be involved in discovering persons who are not Christians, cultivating them, witnessing to them, and leading them to accept Christ as Savior. New Christians and church members not affiliated with a church need the fellowship of a body of believers. This task seeks to involve Sunday School workers and members in reaching such persons for church membership.

Task 4: Minister to Sunday School Members and Nonmembers

The purpose of this task is to involve the Bible teaching program leaders and members in helping one another and those in the church and community. Both crisis and continuing ministries are included, implying that a Christian life-style will be developed and practiced in every class and department throughout the Sunday School.

This important task of ministry is putting into practice the teachings of the Bible. It means every Sunday School member should be encouraged to meet the needs of other persons in the spirit of Christ. This may take the form of personal service, concrete acts of caring expressed in material support, encouraging words, affirmation, or simply taking the time to listen. This task is at the heart of a loving, caring fellowship.

Sunday School leaders should remember that the primary thrust of this task is ministering to persons who are members or are prospects for Sunday School, not specialized target groups within the community.

Task 5: Lead Members to Worship

The purpose of this task is to provide motivation for persons to participate in family and church worship experiences and to

90

provide both motivation and material for personal worship.

It is the responsibility and privilege of the leaders of Sunday School to encourage worship. Spiritual renewal and Christian growth of each member is important to the work of the church. Thus, the Sunday School supports this act of worship through activities that encourage persons to become involved in worship.

Worship includes those experiences designed to help persons feel the presence of the Holy Spirit, express praise to God, reaffirm their commitment to Jesus Christ, and renew their spirits. It is a personal encounter with God in which the Christian experiences a deepening of his faith and strengthening of his commitment to service.

This task is accomplished through three major actions: (1) through providing materials to members to assist them in personal worship. Daily Bible reading and devotional helps such as *Open Windows, Home Life,* and *encounter!* provided through the Sunday School are examples of this action; (2) planning experiences that will motivate persons to worship. In the Sunday School itself and through additional experiences such as retreats, persons are led to worship; (3) promoting opportunities to worship. Since most churches conduct Sunday School before the worship hour on Sunday morning, the Sunday School leaders are provided a regular opportunity to encourage participation in the corporate worship experience.

Task 6: Interpret and Undergird the Work of the Church and the Denomination

The purpose of this task is to present orally, visually, or in printed form the goals, plans, and activities of the church and denomination and explain their significance. A further purpose is to undergird through cooperative support the work of the other programs of the church and denomination. All these efforts should help each Sunday School member to participate in the life and work of the church and denomination.

All programs share this task. Criteria for determining what is to be communicated through the Bible teaching program include the following: (1) the information and program support should be vital to the life and work of the church and/or denomination; (2) the information and program support should be compatible with the church tasks performed by the Bible teaching program; and (3) the information and program support should be in keeping with the age, maturity, and need of the recipients.

Task Exceptions for Certain Bible Teaching Program Approaches

Vacation Bible Schools, Mission Vacation Bible Schools, and Backyard Bible Clubs are approaches for accomplishing the tasks of the Bible teaching program. However, their structure is broader. In addition to the Bible teaching program tasks described here, they also perform some of the tasks of other church programs:

1. Develop musical skills, attitudes, and understandings
2. Witness and minister through music
3. Equip church members in discipleship
4. Teach Christian theology and Baptist doctrine, Christian ethics, Christian history, and church polity and organization
5. Teach missions and engage in missions

These tasks are described in the work of other programs.

These then are the six tasks of the Bible teaching program. Each one is important to the ongoing work of the church; each is needed for a balanced Sunday School program.

How are the tasks of the Bible teaching program accomplished? The remainder of this chapter will be devoted to this question as we look to the practical application of Sunday School work.

SUNDAY SCHOOL IS ORGANIZING TO ACCOMPLISH THE TASK

The work of the Sunday School is important. The tasks of the Bible teaching program as outlined give us a clear picture of the work to be done. How, then, should a church go about doing this important work? At some point each church must decide that this is its work and this is how it will accomplish the task.

The Southern Baptist Sunday School is the clear expression of this work in action. For this reason, organization of the Sunday School is important to the church.

Organization in its simplest form is recognizing that the job is too big for one person to do, so the work is divided into two or more parts. If there is work for five or fifteen or fifty or one hundred, the work is divided through organization. And that's why Sunday Schools have officers who give leadership to departments and classes. It is simply dividing the work to accomplish the total purpose of the Sunday School.

The importance of organization is outlined in the book *Working in Sunday School:*

"Effective organization can be the means of accomplishing this ideal in the church. The Sunday School provides the opportunity for such an organization.

"Louis A. Allen defines organization this way: 'Organization [is] the process of identifying and grouping the work to be performed, defining and delegating responsibility and authority, and establishing relationships for the purpose of enabling people to work most effectively together in accomplishing objectives' [*Management and Organization,* p. 57].

"Applying this principle to the Sunday School, someone has said, 'Organization is placing ourselves in the best possible position to be used by the Holy Spirit.' This definition identifies the real reason for organizing departments and classes, for keeping records and prospect files, for electing officers and holding planning meetings: to be in a position to accomplish God's purposes. This makes it all worthwhile! This gives the Sunday School organization its purpose."[2]

Therefore, every Sunday School needs good organization. Two reasons help us keep this in focus.

1. Organization Is Scriptural

The idea of organization to accomplish a purpose was not originated by Sunday School leaders. In fact, it is the application of the scriptural approach. In the Old Testament Jethro came to the aid of his son-in-law Moses. He taught Moses an important lesson in organization.

"Moreover thou shalt provide out of all the people able men, such as fear God, men of truth, hating covetousness; and place *such* over them, *to be* rulers of thousands, *and* rulers of hundreds, rulers of fifties, and rulers of tens" (Ex. 18:21).

Likewise, the apostle Paul applied sound organizational

93

principles. As he moved out on his famous journeys he trained leaders, left them in charge, and returned later to retrain and encourage them. Paul saw the need to multiply his ministry through organization.

2. Organization Is Logical and Practical

Through the years Sunday School leaders have learned how important it is to apply organization to the Sunday School. Such matters as size of each department and each class, record keeping, the importance of grading by groups, and teaching and reaching people by age developments point up the need for logical organization and practical application of that organization throughout the Sunday School.

SUNDAY SCHOOL IS PERSON CENTERED

Sunday School is a people's movement. The focus of all Sunday School is on each person as he or she is reached for Bible study, taught the Word of God, and led into a faith relationship with Christ. It is also the people of the church who make all of this happen through the Sunday School.

Each year approximately 750,000 people commit themselves to work in Sunday Schools in Southern Baptist churches. With the exception of pastors and staff persons, all of these are volunteers giving themselves without pay to the cause of reaching and teaching other people. Sunday School is dependent upon these people. So the Sunday School places a major emphasis on persons—persons to be reached and persons doing the reaching.

One of the major efforts of the Sunday School is defining the leadership roles to be filled and matching those roles with people in the church. This is accomplished over and over again through helping every Christian discover his or her gifts and using these gifts through the Sunday School. Along with the other church organizations, the Sunday School leaders work to help each person discover how he or she can best be used by God in the service of the church.

Thus, the Sunday School is dependent upon the people who have voluntarily chosen to serve in many different capacities.

Without these people the work of Sunday School, and to a great extent the work of the church, would slow down or perhaps even stop. But many things accomplished are accomplished with the help of these people.

The church must place a major emphasis on leadership enlistment. Each worker must be led to have a clear understanding of his or her purpose for serving in the Sunday School. Along with this clarity of purpose, the worker must be committed and faithful to his cause, dependable, and willing to share in the work of the Sunday School. In addition a positive, enthusiastic spirit is important. A deep sense of dependency on God's leadership is a quality needed in each worker.

These qualities in Sunday School workers are cultivated through training. Southern Baptists have placed a major emphasis on continual training for every leader. Each year most Sunday Schools provide training opportunities of various kinds for their leadership. It is a task never completed and always important.

SUNDAY SCHOOL IS PLANNING AHEAD FOR REACHING AND TEACHING

Another question which must be asked over and over again by Sunday School leaders is, What is our work and how are we going to get it done? Through regular planning this question is answered again and again. Thus, the work of the Sunday School is clearly defined and assigned to workers for accomplishment. Without planning, the work flounders. For this reason several forms of planning are important to the Sunday School.

Annual planning.—The Sunday School director and the Sunday School council (made up of the department directors and other general officers) carry the responsibility for planning one year in advance. Through annual planning, major goals are determined by the council, projects and emphases are decided upon for the coming year, and assignments for these are made. Through annual planning the Sunday School program becomes a part of the church program as these plans are added to the church calendar well in advance.

Monthly planning.—The Sunday School council meets at

least monthly to develop its ongoing plans. As each project and emphasis draws closer, the council plans to see that all the work is completed and plans are communicated throughout the Sunday School to workers and members.

Weekly planning.—Each department in the Sunday School is encouraged to conduct a weekly planning meeting. This meeting is directed by the department director. The importance of weekly planning cannot be overemphasized; it is the heartbeat of effective outreach and Bible teaching.

Four elements are essential for successful weekly planning: (1) There must be a definite commitment to the weekly workers' meeting by the pastor, staff, and Sunday School director; (2) There must be a priority of schedule for the weekly workers' meeting, usually conducted on Wednesday nights. An hour and fifteen minutes is the minimum time needed for effective planning. No other meetings which compete for worker participation should be scheduled during weekly workers' meeting time; (3) There must be a commitment to weekly planning by every Sunday School worker; (4) The department director must be prepared for a purposeful planning session each week. In other words, something good must happen to those who attend if the weekly workers' meeting is to continue to be effective.

SUNDAY SCHOOL IS PROVIDING A SETTING FOR LEARNING

Learning environment is important for effective Bible teaching. Since World War II Southern Baptists have invested millions of dollars in education buildings to provide teaching space. Today, Bible teaching takes place in many different settings. Some are ideal, while others are improvised. In each case, however, the setting for learning is important. The primary emphasis in Sunday School is on individual participation of the learner. For this reason each class needs space that encourages participation. Each Sunday School should work continually to improve space and the teaching setting for each Bible study group.

Closely related to space needs are teaching tools for effective Bible learning. Such things as Bibles, concordances, maps, chalkboards, tables, chairs, record players, and pianos are just a few of the resources needed. It is the rare Sunday School which can purchase everything needed at one time. In most cases equipment must be purchased over a period of time. Sunday School leaders must give constant attention to needed resources in order to continue to improve the Bible learning setting at every age level.

SUNDAY SCHOOL IS REACHING PEOPLE

How do Sunday School leaders apply themselves to this reaching task? By organizing, enlisting, training, planning, and providing a good learning environment. Why? To reach other people with the gospel of Christ. Nothing is more biblical than reaching out and touching individual lives.

Reaching people means people not just like us, but people of different races, backgrounds, cultures, and languages as well. It means reaching persons who do not have sight or hearing, or who are mentally retarded, or who have handicaps. In short, in reaching people, no one should be left out. The Sunday School must address itself to every person, just as Jesus did.

The task of reaching people is accomplished through mobilizing the entire Sunday School to invite every unenlisted person in the community to come to Bible study each week. Visitation to the homes should continue to be the primary means of reaching out. Nothing can take the place of person-to-person contact between Sunday School member and unenlisted people. The Sunday School leaders must work to involve each person in this outreach effort.

Each department and class of the Sunday School should encourage regular contact with prospects through telephoning, letters and cards, and other activities to help each person know the church people want them involved in regular Bible study.

SUNDAY SCHOOL IS TEACHING THE BIBLE

Southern Baptist Sunday Schools are structured to provide effective Bible study on every age level. From the youngest baby in the preschool department to the oldest adult, the intent is to provide the very best Bible teaching on a level that each person can understand.

Bible teaching includes factual learning about the Bible, its people, its times, and its message of God through Jesus Christ. Bible teaching also includes the application of these Bible truths to the lives of each learner. Every worker in the Sunday School should seek to establish a balance between facts and application in their teaching of the Bible.

The textbook for all Sunday School teaching is the Bible— God's revelation to man. The Sunday School Department of the Baptist Sunday School Board provides many support materials to assist the teachers. Through these materials the churches choose their approach to Bible study, their curriculum plan. But these are to support the teachers in teaching the Book—the Bible.

Undergirding this Bible teaching is the power of God's Spirit. The teacher of the Bible is not alone. The Holy Spirit is the teacher, also. When we teach the Bible, we rely upon the Holy Spirit to enlighten, guide, and direct what takes place in each classroom. This is the genius of Bible teaching in Sunday School. It is God's plan for sharing the good news.

SUNDAY SCHOOL IS LEADING PERSONS TO FAITH IN CHRIST

Sunday School and personal witnessing go together. The primary means of faith sharing is through the Sunday School. Sunday School witnessing has been defined as "the people of God actively seeking out unredeemed persons; sharing concern for them; teaching them God's truths through Bible study; and leading them, under the influence of the Holy Spirit, into a faith relationship with God through Jesus Christ."[3]

A close analysis of this definition reveals the important ingredients in a witnessing Sunday School.

1. Witnessing Is the Work of the People of God
Telling others about Christ is not the exclusive business of the ordained ministry or a few devoted persons in the church. The

Bible teaches that witnessing is the responsibility of all Christians. Sunday School departments and classes provide the climate for each person to be an active witness. The study group is at the heart of active witnessing because it establishes personal relationships, it has continuing ministries, and it is active throughout the year.

2. Witnessing Is Sharing Concern, Teaching, and Leading Others to Faith in Christ

Reaching people for Bible study is important, but leading them to faith in Christ is even more so. The work of the Sunday School is incomplete until the leaders and workers follow through by sharing their faith. This should happen all during the year as Christians say to those who don't know Christ as Savior: "I have experienced Jesus Christ in personal faith and he is my Savior. He can be yours, too. Let me share this good news with you."

The essence of the work of the Sunday School is to provide a climate for continual personal witnessing in the class session and throughout the week.

SUNDAY SCHOOL IS INVOLVING MEMBERS IN LIVING THE GOSPEL

Living the gospel is the completion of the Great Commission: "Teaching them to observe all that I have commanded you" (Matt. 28:20, RSV).[4] This is the class actively involved in ministry to persons. Sunday School leaders must feel the responsibility to lead each member to apply the truths to life. The Bible is not adequately taught and learned until its concepts and principles are applied to daily living. Every Sunday School department and class provides a group for accomplishing these ministries through group as well as individual effort.

Ministry and application of truths to life take many forms. It is sharing through giving the cup of cold water in Christ's name. It is helping persons through sickness and grief. It is providing support in times of family crisis. Whatever the need, the Christian, the Sunday School member, and the group must be prepared to respond in Christian love. The Sunday School is the expression of

99

Christ's love. It is the church involved in ministry to persons.

SUNDAY SCHOOL IS ADMINISTERING THROUGH THE HOLY SPIRIT

None of these principles that are essential to Sunday School work can be implemented without depending on the Spirit of God. Each worker in the Sunday School should seek God's will in all that is done in the church. Submission to God's will and a willingness to follow the leadership of his Spirit is imperative for every Sunday School worker.

Unless the Holy Spirit comes to anoint, bless, empower, and direct the work of Christ, his mission will not be accomplished. Sunday School teachers, directors, outreach leaders, and members must recognize the need for God's power in their lives. With the Spirit of God leading and teaching through the Sunday School, there is no limit to what can be accomplished for Jesus Christ.

---

1. W. L. Howse and W. O. Thomason, *A Dynamic Church* (Nashville: Convention Press, 1969), pp. 46-48.
2. A. V. Washburn and Donald F. Trotter, comps., *Working in Sunday School* (Nashville: Convention Press, 1974), p. 32.
3. Max L. Caldwell, comp., *Witness to Win* (Nashville: Convention Press, 1978), p. 21.
4. From the Revised Standard Version of the Bible, copyrighted 1946, 1952, © 1971, 1973.

Chapter 8

Equipping for Responsible Discipleship

The Church Training program of a church takes its mandate from Ephesians. This New Testament book gives us a grand design for individual and corporate spiritual health. In Ephesians the doctrine of the church reaches its highest point. The ultimate goal of Christian growth and maturity is placed in the context of the eternal purposes of God and the place of Christ and his people in that purpose. W. O. Carver has called Ephesians "The Supreme Document." Just as the people of the Reformation discovered the book of Romans as a guide for their life and times, perhaps we are rediscovering the epistle to the Ephesians as a letter speaking directly to churches that are concerned about discipleship.

Ephesians 4:11-16 sets forth the major themes of Christian discipleship. It calls us to reshape our personal lives and our lives as they relate to others according to biblical patterns. It provides us with a basic expression of equipping the saints, personal Christian growth, doctrinal integrity, and the ultimate goal of upbuilding the church.

In this "grand idea" the three words that outline a church's program of discipleship are found. These three words suggest an equipping, growing, and building program of training. Personal and corporate spiritual vitality go together. It is impossible to grow to full stature as an individual while separated from the smaller and larger groups within the church. At the same time the full body of believers cannot grow without the renewing of its members.

A church on mission will be concerned with the spiritual revitalization of its members as instruments through which God works in the world. If our hearts and minds are not properly transformed, we are like musicians with good music and expensive instruments but playing out of tune. Only an awakened people in an awakened church will serve as a base for a church on mission during the next decade.

AN EQUIPPING MINISTRY

Christian disciples are directed toward two kinds of ministry. One is a ministry of making disciples of all the nations (Matt. 28:18-20). The other is an edifying ministry within the body of Christ. Each member plays a part in the building up of that body until it attains "the measure of the stature of the fulness of Christ" (Eph. 4:13).

Ephesians 4:7 suggests that God provides for the growth of the church through gifts to his people. These gifts are special energies and capacities for service. Every Christian has a gift of some kind. Each person has a capacity for service somewhere within the body of Christ. There is a wide diversity of gifts, but they should blend in purpose and harmony. The purpose of these gifts is outlined in Ephesians 4:12: "for the equipment of the saints, for the work of ministry, for building up the body of Christ." (RSV)[1]

The aim of Christ's gifts is introduced in the "equipping of the saints." The word *katartidzo* is rich in the imagery of training. In Luke 6:40 we read, "A pupil is not above his teacher; but everyone, after he has been fully trained [*katartismenos*], will be like his teacher" (NASB).[2] Here this Greek word carries the significance of "fully trained for a task." The saints are to be completely fitted out for tasks of ministry. The word for equipping carries with it the tasks of training, preparation, education, and discipline.

This equipping will provide each of the saints of God with a service or ministry. The various gifts are given by Christ to unite, prepare, equip, and train the saints to fulfill the ministry each is to receive. The equipping task organizes and mobilizes Christians for mission.

But this is not all. The ultimate work of this ministry is "for upbuilding the body of Christ." Christ has given the gifts for the purpose of providing the necessary equipment for all to engage in the task of ministry to his body, the church. *Oikodome,* or "building up," is spiritual edification which consists of everything that develops our spiritual lives.

A church's training program will provide plans and resources for an equipping ministry in doctrine, family life, witnessing, personal Christian growth, church and community issues, leadership training, and many other content areas. The purpose of these plans and resources is to "fully outfit" the people of God for every good work.

A GROWING MINISTRY

Fully equipped for our task of ministering, we are to work until all attain full Christian maturity (Eph. 4:12). The expression *attaining* is used often in the book of Acts for travelers reaching their designation. This word suggests that Christian progress is a journey toward maturity (Acts 13:51; 16:1; 18:19). Paul significantly refers to "the whole number" of Christians. In our work of ministry, we are to neglect no person. All should arrive at the goal of spiritual maturity. In a sense this never ends because new generations of children, youth, and new believers require our ministry. *Growing* is one of Paul's favorite terms for spiritual progress. Full-grown maturity is the goal for all believers—new Christians, those who have shown some progression in their faith, and others who have lagged behind.

A church's training program will offer planned sequences of personal growth and discipleship for all church members. Growth in discipleship will lead to daily disciplines in Bible study and prayer, living under the lordship of Christ, bearing fruit in witness and ministry, and weekly involvement with God's people in active church membership. Ongoing church training groups for all ages provide the best settings for growing Christian disciples.

The hindrances to personal Christian growth are outlined in Ephesians 4:14. This passage gives a graphic description of the helplessness of infants. They are helpless because they have not been fitted out properly with the word of truth. The importance of doctrine is clearly stated by Paul. True doctrine provides each believer with the foundations of faith because the truths it expresses offer stability. But every human doctrine is like wind—unstable and transient, causing drifting and instability.

Immature Christians also hinder the growth of the church by their gullibility and instability. Those Christians not grounded in doctrine become easy prey for the peddlers of religious fads and heresies. They are vulnerable to every idle suggestion and every religious novelty. Churches pay a heavy price by not grounding their people in doctrinal truth.

Christians can no longer cling to a state of infancy. This is Paul's favorite theme to illustrate a lack of understanding of doctrine. Paul's contrasts between "infants" and "maturity" is illustrated in 1 Corinthians 1-3. In the infant there is only the capacity for elementary instruction, but those who are mature are capable of digesting the solid food of doctrine.

Truth is to be spoken and lived in love. The authentic Christian lives his faith in an atmosphere of love. This phrase, "speaking the truth in love" (Eph. 4:15), is a norm of Christian ethics and of spiritual progress. It is mainly through the principle of love that Christians grow.

This "striving toward wholeness" is both individual and corporate. The believer's response is both a beginning and continuing struggle, both a birth and a growth. The goal of the Christian life is personal and relational. It cannot be reduced to static achievement. It remains both a dying and a resurrecting, self-forgetting and a self-realizing, a "becoming as a child" as well as a "coming of age."

A BUILDING UP MINISTRY

The equipping, growing, and building up tasks found in Ephesians 4:11-16 focus on the church as an organism designed by God for discipling and growth. The "building up" image is God's design for church growth. The idea of "build up" rests on the New Testament concept of the church as the house, the temple, and the building of God. According to 1 Peter 2:5, this "spiritual house" is built up through "living stones." This same thought underlies Paul's description of the church as the temple of God (Eph. 2:21). The building up theme of Ephesians 4 incorporates the entire work of increasing the outward number and the inward faith of the congregation. Growth is seen as both personal and corporate. It combines the inner building with the strong outward growth that multiplied in numbers. This summary of growth is found in Acts 9:31: "And so it was that the church throughout Judea, Galilee, and Samaria had a time of peace. Through the help of the Holy Spirit it was strengthened and grew in numbers, as it lived in reverence for the Lord" (GNB).[3]

It is for the sake of upbuilding that God equips the church with a variety of gifts and ministries. The entire process of up-building is directed toward the growth, maturity, and adulthood of the church. It is of utmost importance for the upbuilding that the church receive and learn about Christ (Eph. 4:20-21). It is through learning Christ that the church is safeguarded against instability and the deceit of false doctrine (Eph. 4:14).

Upbuilding is a continuing work of God with his people. This building process is dynamic. It is the point of departure but also the goal. Everyone in Christ is built up together in this building. The interaction of the members of the church is in connection with love. Paul twice uses the words *in love* in Ephesians 4:15-16. An abundant and generous spiritual supply of love to each other provides motivation for the upbuilding. Paul is saying that we are to build up the body, the church, and do this with loving hearts.

A training program's small-group structure provides the ve-hicle for growth. The principle of body growth is found in the smaller cell-like structures that offer shared life and belonging. It is through these groups that people become involved with Christ and with one another, increase connective ties that build up the body, and accept leadership roles and tasks. This principle is the same for churches of all sizes.

THE WORK OF THE CHURCH TRAINING PROGRAM

The training program of a church is concerned with equip-ping all God's people for the work of Christian service, to build up the body of Christ (Eph. 4:12). These biblical mandates provide a pattern of equipping, growing, and building up ministries through new church member training, church member training, and church leader training.

105

With the equipping, growing, and building up challenges of Ephesians providing the biblical base, the Church Training program seeks to equip church members and leaders in four tasks.

Task 1: Equip Church Members for Discipleship and Personal Ministry

An equipping ministry will prepare church members for a life of discipleship. Discipleship is the Christian's understanding of the dynamics of spiritual life. It is the Christian's lifelong commitment to the person, teaching, and spirit of Jesus Christ. Living under Jesus' lordship involves progressive learning, growth in Christlikeness, application of biblical truth, sharing a living faith, and responsible church membership. Discipleship in the New Testament was a radical decision to follow Jesus. This meant that the disciple, the follower of Jesus, witnessed the words of Jesus, heard the words of Jesus, and revealed the ministry of Jesus to others. Being with Jesus resulted in his participation in a work similar to that of Jesus.

Jesus taught the disciples to be loyal to him. In Mark 4:11, he told them, "To you has been given the secret to the kingdom of God" (RSV). On many occasions he took them aside to teach them the inner meaning of a parable that he had spoken to the crowd. But the things that he taught were not just to be learned and passed on. They were to be learned and lived. Discipleship always receives its focus in Jesus and his concern for people.

The Christian disciple is both concerned with personal Christian growth and the corporate growth of the entire body. It is not enough for persons to grow. Individual Christians are not ends in themselves; they are cells in the living body of Christ. Authentic discipleship involves both personal growth and the growth of the church as a whole. Each church member should be instructed in witnessing, the personal discipline of prayer, a productive relationship with the larger Christian community, a supportive and nurturing relationship with a small group, and doctrinal and ethical stability.

The growth of the new church member is a priority concern. Young converts are like new life intended to quicken and freshen the body of older Christians. At the same time the larger Christian community offers stability and direction to new Christians. If new waves of converts do not receive sound instruction, they become dormant and ineffective Christian witnesses.

An adequate program of new member training will provide opportunities for both the church and the new member to affirm their relationships and commitment to each other.

New Christians should immediately be involved in a personal growth program of discipleship. This will include a daily discipline of personal study, devotion, and prayer. They need to experience a warm relationship with a new family, the body of Christ. They need to understand the nature of salvation and the power of walking in newness of life. They need to see the Bible as a source of authority for their lives. They need to accept their responsibility to witness to others about Jesus Christ.

Counseling sessions will help new members understand their conversion and commitment to Christ. Each new member needs opportunities to express to others his understandings and feelings about his conversion experience. Parents of young converts need guidance in understanding their children's experience and in nurturing their spiritual development.

As new members come to understand these basics of the Christian life, they can move into the deeper aspects of church membership. This can be accomplished through sessions dealing with the church and its covenant, its belief, its history, and its program and organization. Effective new church member training should lead new members to get involved in the life and work of their church. An understanding of their spiritual gifts will help them find outlets for ministry.

Church members need to be instructed in the personal skills of discipleship. These are the competencies and abilities that will help them live the Christian life effectively. Equipping persons for discipleship results in competence—their ability to relate skills to calling in an effective way. Competence means that there is a sufficient supply of what a person needs to meet the demands of ministry. Knowledge, judgment, and skill are some of these competencies.

The disciples were far from being equipped when Jesus left them to go to his Father. But they discovered that what they had was sufficient with the addition of the Holy Spirit. Jesus had taught them the lessons of the kingdom—prayer, freedom, the nature of holiness, the pilgrimage of faith, the private and corporate life, and the meaning of servanthood.

Jesus' expectation of competence in his disciples included several things. He expected his disciples to bear fruit. But he also expected many good works of high quality. Competence and skill consist not only of an enduring permanence that produces much but an excellence that shows itself in quality. Disciples of Jesus need two qualities—diligence and patience. The first insures quantity, and the second produces superior quality.

Discipleship promises growth. Daily growth in discipleship skills is essential. There are many skills that the disciple should develop, but these skills can be categorized in four areas. Disciples should grow in their ability to feel and respond to the presence of God (worship), to share in word and deed what Christ has done and continues to do in their lives (proclaim and witness), to respond warmly to the needs of others (minister), and to follow a program of continued equipping and training (nurture and educate).

Task 2: Teach Christian Theology and Baptist Doctrine, Christian Ethics, Christian History, and Church Polity and Organization

Many Christians are influenced by worldly patterns of thinking, motivation, and behavior. The result is a spiritual life that lacks depth and vitality. Individuals and churches must become aware of the danger of conforming to the world. This is an awesome task that requires an experience with the truths of Holy Scripture. To teach doctrine, ethics, church history, and church polity is to develop in the minds of Christians the concepts that are consistent with biblical truth.

The study of doctrine establishes church members in the truths of Scripture. It helps Christians organize their beliefs into a personal theology. A church member who "thinks biblically" is able to organize his beliefs and reflect these beliefs in personal attitudes and daily actions. The principles of the Bible, under the Holy Spirit's illumination, act as a clarifying lens through which we view and interpret all things. Doctrinal truth is essential as a foundation for all church ministries.

The Christian needs assistance in making decisions about

how he will live in this world. Once Christians have been exposed to the truths of authentic faith, they can move out from themselves to give attention to God and others. Then they can think and pray about the critical issues that face the church and society. There are many patterns of living today which border on idolatry. The current trends in moral codes, technology, educational patterns, sexual pursuits, racial and ethnic allegiances, and economic and government structures exert a constant pressure on the Christian. These forces require decisions every day. Growing in our understanding of Christian ethics helps us as authentic disciples to respond to these worldly pressures.

Christian history tells a story of God's dealings with the human race as he revealed himself in Christ. It includes the biblical witness to the early development of the church. It reveals the doctrinal, moral, and ethical triumphs and defeats of Christians and churches as a part of all that God has done through the Christian movement. Through our connections with Christians of all ages, we are able to see ourselves in the total context of what God is doing in the world.

An understanding of church polity and organization gives us insight into the larger network of Christians. Our discipleship is expressed in the context of one local church in one specific denomination. We need to understand how Baptists organize to do God's work. We must constantly seek to organize our churches in light of our understanding of the biblical patterns. This is the task of church polity and organization.

Task 3: Equip Church Leaders for Service

Most leadership theory is associated with concepts of power, control, authority, and dominance. The leader is at the apex of the pyramid. Everyone else is underneath. These are pedestal concepts. The leader is usually thought of as a person who is higher and better than all those beneath him. The leader controls, manages, and dominates. Others follow, work, serve, and obey.

When Jesus observed this theory in action, he saw jealousy and unproductive striving. He was compelled to say, "This is not how it is to be among you." Christ taught us a different model of leadership. The greatest person is the one who faithfully serves in the place of need; who uses gifts to bless, help, enrich, and minister without regard to recognition, honor, position, or power. Jesus turned the pyramid upside down. He said that the first shall be last, and the greatest shall be the servant of all.

The leadership style of a Christian should never set him apart or inject division into the fellowship. It solidifies and knits together the community of faith as one body. Each Christian should contribute according to his gifts. All should be grateful to God for the service others can render.

Moses had a gift of leadership. When he came down from the mountain, the people recognized his power to lead. His face was shining with the reflection of the one who had spoken to him. His heartbeat had become the heartbeat of God. Moses led others not on the basis of his talents or abilities. His right to lead grew out of his total obedience to the call of God.

Servant leadership is based on the assumption that each person has his own special gift. "Each has his own special gift from God, one of one kind and one of another. . . . Let every one lead the life which the Lord has assigned to him, and in which God has called him" (1 Cor. 7:7,17, RSV). The gift is bestowed on persons to be used for the good of others. It is not a natural talent but a call of grace and a call to service. Gifts are given to enable us to contribute to the growth of other Christians. The power to grow into spiritual maturity is given by the Spirit through one another. "The Spirit's presence is shown in some way in each person for the good of all" (1 Cor. 12:7, GNB).

Our gifts should find direct outward expression through our church responsibilities. This is a two-fold responsibility. Church leaders must help persons find ways of using their gifts through opportunities of service that already exist. Persons with gifts must find ways of using their gifts in the service of Christ.

The church member who leads through service finds himself operating on two fronts. First, there is a spontaneous show of the Spirit's moving in his life with a recognition that the Spirit of God has given him gifts. Second, each church member must find ways to let his gifts be expressed through the church.

Gifts need forms through which to express themselves. Each Christian must relate his gifts to the structures of the church. The Spirit of God does not necessarily change our responsibilities.

But he gives these tasks new dimensions. Letting our gifts flow through our tasks gives our work an added power. It makes our church responsibilities less a burden and more a joyful expression of Christian ministry.

In our church work we become aware of a strong spiritual presence that is powerful enough to transform our gifts in tangible expressions through our responsibilities. Whether we help the needy or preach, build fellowship or teach, maintain the buildings or care for the burdened, we should do all our work in a way that builds up the church and provides an environment of growth for other Christians.

In training church leaders a church should analyze its needs and call out persons with the gifts that are needed. Training enhances, sharpens, and illuminates a person's gifts. The task of equipping church leaders includes training potential leaders, giving them basic job training, and orienting them in general leadership skills.

Potential leader training should be offered to older youth and adults who are not yet enlisted to serve in specific places of leadership in the church. It helps people identify and evaluate their leadership skills.

Basic job training enables a person to function in a specific leadership role. This training is conducted in cooperation with other church programs.

General leadership training enables a person to develop as a leader, beyond the point of being able to function simply in a given job. General leader training enhances and deepens a church member's leadership skills.

In all leadership positions in the church, servanthood is the model. This model is found uniquely in the New Testament. It is modeled after Jesus Christ and the servant nature of his body, the church.

Task 4: Interpret and Undergird the Work of the Church and the Denomination

The mandate of Christ to make disciples calls for a worldwide ministry. Growing Christians and churches will minister in a broad network of relationships. Baptist churches fulfill their mission by cooperative efforts locally and around the world.

These cooperative relationships include the association, the state convention, and the Southern Baptist Convention.

It is important that Baptists work together toward worthy objectives. Coordination and cooperation are possible only when the lines of communication between church members and leaders and denominational leaders are kept open. Performance of this task helps church members participate more meaningfully in the life and work of their church and denomination.

THE SETTINGS FOR TRAINING

Individuals and small groups are cells in the larger body, the church. The settings for training require three essential elements: learners, leaders, and resources. These elements could be placed in the form of a triangle. The triangle represents people interacting with other people, leaders, and resources.

All church members should be involved in training. The task of equipping is clear from the New Testament mandate. Churches should take seriously the necessity of equipping all God's people. All church members have needs, intentions, and goals. All church members are learners. In some way, at some level, all church members should be involved in a setting that equips them for ministry. These settings will vary according to a church's size. But these principles of equipping God's people apply in every church situation.

Leaders are servants, working among learners and modeling as clearly as possible the concepts which they are teaching. Leaders are elected according to the church's plan. A leader may be a resource himself, or he may provide resources. A leader may be a facilitator or a coordinator of learning with a number of people. A leader uses his or her gifts to assist people in Christian growth. At times leaders and learners will be equally involved as peers in the learning process.

The third element in a learning setting is resources. Both learner and leader interact with resources in a variety of ways and at various levels of intensity. A Church Training program should provide resources for both learners and leaders.

Any place that meets the requirements of interaction between learner, leader, and resources becomes a setting for training. Learning settings are opportunities for a church member to get involved in training. Churches of all sizes and all cultural backgrounds should seek to have a continuing ministry of new member, member, and leader training.

Much of the training will be done on Sunday evening before or after the evening worship hour. This is a prime time in most churches. The importance of this time and its relationship to the evening worship service must not be minimized or overlooked. But training must be done at times other than Sunday evening. A church may discover that all times and many places are valid settings for meeting the training needs of the church membership.

Ephesians 4:11-16 provides a valid biblical model of spiritual life for Christians. The equipping, growing, and building up dynamic of church life is clearly presented in this passage. All churches on mission will follow the principles of this grand design for a vital training ministry.

Chapter 9

Extending Christ's Ministry at Home and Abroad

A church on mission in the eighties must be true to the Commission of Christ: "Go, then, to all peoples everywhere," he declared, "and make them my disciples: baptize them in the name of the Father, the Son, and the Holy Spirit, and teach them to obey everything I have commanded you. And I will be with you always, to the end of the age" (Matt. 28:19-20, GNB).[1]

To achieve this commission, a church must have a missionary vision. It must minister the love of Christ to people in its own community as well as around the world. Missionary vision in a church is nurtured by its emphasis on Christian stewardship and establishing new churches as well as its promotion and support of Woman's Missionary Union and Brotherhood.

WOMAN'S MISSIONARY UNION

A church's missions responsibility begins in its community and extends throughout the world. In accepting Christ's challenge to go into all the world, churches have organized to do their work. Woman's Missionary Union is a church organization for women, girls, and preschool children. This organization is committed to helping a church achieve its full potential. It does its work through four tasks.

Task 1: Teach Missions

The church must always assign a high significance to the ministry of teaching, since this was central in the life and work of Jesus. The study of missions, one part of the total curriculum of Southern Baptist churches, is one of the most challenging of all educational opportunities in a church. The in-depth study of missions helps a church achieve its reason for being, encourages church members to understand their world responsibility, cultivates concern, and motivates the investment of life and resources in missions.

In teaching missions, this organization leads persons to explore with growing understanding the nature, implications, and evidences of God's missionary purpose and to respond to that purpose in personal commitment and obedience.

Content for teaching missions includes the biblical basis of Christian missions, the progress of Christian missions, contemporary missions, and the spiritual development of the learner.

Feeling that any understanding of missions must be based on biblical concepts, Woman's Missionary Union centers its study on the missionary message of the Bible.

From the study of missions history one learns how far churches have progressed in carrying out the Great Commission. This helps one understand the plans and methods of contemporary missions.

A large proportion of the study time in organizations is given to learning about contemporary missions. It is important for members to know what the missions boards are doing in fulfilling their obligation to the churches of the Southern Baptist Convention. WMU provides information on the geographic areas where missionaries are serving, including progress of work, trends, and factors influencing missions work.

The spiritual development of the learner is a significant part of teaching missions. The WMU member is led to discover the meaning of prayer, personal meditation, stewardship, mission action and personal witnessing, and of career and noncareer mission service. The role of women is also studied.

Age-level organizations provide a ready-made setting for the teaching of missions. In addition, special study projects are promoted for individuals, families, and the congregation.

God's work in the world is personalized through missions education. After a person has studied in-depth about missions, she will probably feel a desire to become involved in missions. Two tasks provide persons with opportunities to express actively the concern they feel through study.

Task 2: Engage in Mission Action and Personal Witnessing

This task has two prongs—mission action and personal witnessing.

116

Mission action.—Mission action is ministering and witnessing to persons of special need or circumstance who are not members of the church or its programs. Mission action is also combating social and moral problems.

Mission action is the tangible expression of a church's belief that all persons need God and must come to him through Jesus Christ. Mission action represents a church's concern for persons outside its membership.

Mission action includes ministry and witness. The two ideas cannot be separated. Jesus set the example for ministering to people. He made service a significant part of his teachings. He taught that being a neighbor included a deed of service. Likewise Christians are to discover ways to minister to persons.

The content of mission action includes both persons in target groups and target issues. Some of the persons of special need or circumstance to whom a church ministers are prisoners, military personnel, alcoholics, drug abusers, poor, unchurched groups, language groups, internationals, migrants, travelers and tourists, nonreaders, aging, unwed parents, juvenile delinquents, the sick, nonevangelicals, and minority groups.

Target issues are social and moral problems which victimize persons, such as family problems, gambling, pornography, obscenity, alcoholism, drug abuse, racial problems, economic and political problems.

Personal witnessing.—Personal witnessing is a Christian's sharing the gospel of Jesus Christ with another person and encouraging that person to confess Jesus Christ as Savior and Lord.

Fulfilling Christ's commandment to go into all the world compels a church to engage in personal witnessing. As we motivate and train Christ's disciples to do the things Christ has commanded, we are energizing the ministry of witness.

The content of personal witnessing is the message conveyed. It includes the facts of gospel history: God created and rules the universe. He created and loves people, though they have chosen to rebel against God's control in their lives. Through history, God worked out a plan to bring individuals back into fellowship with him. That plan culminated in God's sending his Son. This fellowship is restored when a person accepts what Christ has done and gives control of his life back to God.

Personal witnessing, as programmed by Woman's Missionary Union, is performed by individuals for individuals, but it may be sponsored by organizations and groups. In engaging persons in these actions, Woman's Missionary Union helps develop in them a response to their responsibility to proclaim the gospel and to minister to human need in Christ's name in all the world.

Task 3: Support Missions

A church has the responsibility for supporting the representative missions programs in the associations, state conventions, and Southern Baptist Convention.

Praying, giving, emphasizing the need for persons to become involved in mission service, and providing personal ministries for missionaries and their families designate the major types of support needed by the representative missions programs.

Prayer and missions are inseparably linked. Praying for missions is communication with God in behalf of missionaries and missions work. Every church has a responsibility to help its members become aware of the potential of prayer and to provide opportunities for this experience. Praying for missionaries is one way persons can "go into all the world."

The Week of Prayer for Foreign Missions and the Week of Prayer for Home Missions and the seasons of prayer for state and associational missions are special prayer projects. Persons are encouraged to use the missionary prayer calendar daily.

Giving to missions provides financial support of missions work being conducted for churches by representative programs.

Persons are encouraged to give through the local church. The emphasis on giving in Woman's Missionary Union includes tithing and the Cooperative Program as well as giving to the special missions offerings.

Emphasizing the need for persons to become involved in career and noncareer mission service includes helping to create an environment in which persons can hear and respond to God's call and encouraging and guiding persons who feel God's call to mission service. The emphasis on career and noncareer mission service is designed to help church members find a direct, personal involvement in representative missions work.

118

The need for persons to become involved in career and non-career mission service is emphasized in regular meetings.

Providing personal ministries for missionaries and their families includes words of encouragement and acts of human kindness, such as letter, calls, caring for children and parents, making transportation and housing available, and providing other ministries as needed. This allows churches to keep in touch with missionaries and feel they have a responsibility for the personal well-being of missionaries.

This mission support task links a church with missions efforts around the world.

Task 4: Interpret and Undergird the Work of the Church and the Denomination

Woman's Missionary Union shares this task with all other basic programs. This task means making persons aware of the work of the church and the denomination. WMU serves the church by acting as a channel through which information flows.

Persons receive information and interpretation through ongoing and short-term study, action, and support activities conducted in organizations, in groups, by individuals, families, and congregations.

Woman's Missionary Union works closely with other basic organizations and with the pastor and church staff to help the church fulfill the mission for which Christ established it. Woman's Missionary Union encourages church members to use their influence in helping churches see missions needs at home and abroad and to respond to those needs.

BROTHERHOOD

Brotherhood accomplishes its assignment in the church through the Baptist Men's program for men eighteen years of age and older and through the Royal Ambassador program for boys in grades 1-12. The purpose of Baptist Men and Royal Ambassadors is to equip every man and boy to become a participant in the church as a life-style missionary.

In accordance with the mission purpose of the church, the tasks of Brotherhood work are carried out in six areas of missions performance: (1) internal areas, (2) expansion areas, (3) extension areas, (4) bridging areas, (5) sending areas, and (6) voice to the world.

The internal areas are inside the church. In the internal areas of mission performance, persons are encouraged to discover what gifts and talents God has given them for the benefit of the church and its mission. The church affirms these gifts by entrusting missions activities to individuals.

The area of expansion includes what the church does to reach out in its community to bring the unreached into a saving knowledge of Jesus Christ.

Extension is the process of planting a Christian witness in a new area. Extension begins with a knowledge of a field to which the witness needs to be carried.

Crossing bridges in mission work requires that the church extend its witness to persons in special need and circumstances. Perhaps they speak another language or are of a different sociological or economic group.

An additional area of missions work is that of sending. There are missionaries from mission agencies of the Southern Baptist Convention who have found a calling to give their lives in full-time missionary service.

The church is also a voice to the world and speaks to issues and needs, such as hunger.

In order for the church to meet the responsibilities of missions involvement, it must organize its fellowship in such a way that its purposes are accomplished. It will need organizations for the development of men and boys. One such organization is the Brotherhood program of the church.

The purpose of Brotherhood work is to inform, motivate, and involve men and boys in praying, studying, enlisting, giving, ministering, and bearing witness of Christ in their community and to their world. Brotherhood accomplishes its work in the church through five tasks.

Task 1: Engage in Missions Activities

Missions activities include mission action, personal evangelism, mass evangelism, and special missions projects. Mission action is ministering and witnessing to persons in special need or circumstances who are not members of the church or its programs. Mission action is also combating social and moral problems. Mission action opportunities of the church are limited only by the creative imagination and energy of Christians.

Mission action most often begins as a part of the internal area of performance of the local church, but it quickly grows to the expansion, extension, and bridging areas.

Personal evangelism, or witnessing communicated from one person to another person, is the major way the gospel has been carried across the centuries.

It was Simon Peter, won by personal evangelism, who would later demonstrate the possibilities of mass evangelism by preaching on the day of Pentecost when 3,000 persons were saved.

There are special missions projects which are short-term activities, such as survey and visitation and opportunities for special projects such as disaster relief both at home and on foreign mission fields.

Task 2: Teach Missions

To teach means to stimulate and guide learners in their personal growth. It is imperative that participants in missions activities give adequate study to meaning and methods of mission.

Missions education is that part of Christian education which is concerned with the lifelong development of understandings, attitudes, and skills which will involve persons in carrying out the missions tasks of the church.

The content to be dealt with in teaching missions includes the missionary message of the Bible, the progress of Christian missions, and contemporary missions.

The major emphasis in teaching contemporary missions includes the context in which missions work is done, philosophy of Christian missions, Southern Baptist mission strategy and work, and the missions work of other Christian groups.

In teaching contemporary missions, the major emphasis should be on local church support of worldwide missions through prayer and giving, and especially on providing career and short-term missionary personnel.

All church members should learn about missions. The teaching of missions may take place in the church building, in homes, camps, retreats, and assembly conferences. Missions teaching and learning also takes place as men and boys engage in missions activities.

One of the most important qualities in teaching missions is persistence. The person who teaches missions must have a total commitment to the value of missions education in witnessing and ministering for our Lord.

Task 3: Pray for and Give to Missions

Christ not only taught us to pray for ourselves and others in personal relationships; he also prayed for those whom he sent into the world. Prayer is an element of personal growth. It prepares us to do what Christ has commissioned us to do.

The task of praying for and giving to missions relates to local missions and to "representative" missions. Prayer links churches with missions efforts throughout the world. Prayer is the Christian's way of acknowledging that divine resources are essential to effective missions work.

Giving allows persons to support missions with their financial resources. The Brotherhood gives major emphasis to promoting the Cooperative Program. The Cooperative Program makes it possible to support Southern Baptist institutions and missions agencies through giving.

In addition to the Cooperative Program, two major special offerings, the Lottie Moon Christmas Offering for foreign missions and the Annie Armstrong Easter Offering for home missions, are collected in the churches each year. The Brotherhood organization supports these offerings in the churches and works with WMU in this promotion.

Giving to missions is not simply a Brotherhood task but is a way persons grow in being missionaries. It is also a way of helping to fulfill the Great Commission.

Task 4: Develop Personal Ministry

Develop personal ministry means to discover and implement a service to others which a person is uniquely and spiritually gifted to perform.

This task rests on the concept that each Christian has a call to ministry, and therefore, a gift for putting this ministry into practice. Helping persons discover and channel their individual gifts includes helping them to understand what it means to be called to ministry. They must also be led to call forth their gifts so they can perform their ministry on behalf of the whole body of Christ.

To call forth gifts is to recognize that there are strengths, qualities, and talents in persons and that they are God-given so that the church may fulfill its task of ministry and witness.

The apostle Paul said: "Each one of us has received a special gift in proportion to what Christ has given. . . . It was he who 'gave gifts to mankind'; he appointed some to be apostles, others to be prophets, others to be evangelists, others to be pastors and teachers. He did this to prepare all God's people for the work of Christian service in order to build up the body of Christ" (Eph. 4:7-12, GNB).

An important part of personal ministry development is encouraging pastors in their equipping ministry. This includes providing support, resources, opportunities, and affirmation as pastors equip and enable others to discover, discipline, and channel their individual gifts. Another part of personal ministry development is the affirmation of persons involved in the personal ministry process by the pastor and other members of the fellowship.

Task 5: Interpret and Undergird the Work of the Church and the Denomination

Brotherhood helps persons to understand and support the work of the church and denomination. Accomplishing this objective should result in more meaningful participation in the life and work of the church, association, state convention, and Southern Baptist Convention.

The Brotherhood may also provide organization and leadership for special projects and ministries such as world mission conferences, lay renewal events, visitation, stewardship, enlistment, transportation, and work projects.

MISSIONS OUTREACH THROUGH ESTABLISHING NEW CHURCHES

Christ chose the local church as his instrument to evangelize the world. Human experience and logic have verified the scrip-

123

tural truth that the local church is the most effective means of reaching people with the gospel. If Christians banded together in a local church do not do God's work, no one will.

The writer of 1 Peter points out, "Ye are a chosen generation, a royal priesthood, an holy nation, a peculiar people: that ye should shew forth the praises of him who hath called you out of darkness into his marvelous light. Which in time past were not a people, but are now the people of God: which had not obtained mercy, but now have obtained mercy."

The cutting edge—the point of thrust—in missions is church planting. Ministry, education, and training follow the birth of a church. To be a Christian on mission centers in the congregation. To be involved in church planting today is to be at the very heart of missions.

The responsibility for starting new churches should be assigned to the church missions committee. If the church does not have this committee, it should select one. The committee should have five to seven members, including representatives from the WMU, Brotherhood, and Sunday School. The duties of the committee are listed in chapter 11. The chairman of this committee should be the most competent, mission-minded person in the church. He or she should not be burdened with other church responsibilities. An aggressive program of church planting will demand a lot of work from this committee.

1. Orienting the Church Missions Committee

As soon as the chairman is selected, he or she should contact the chairman of the associational missions committee and the director of associational missions. The chairman should arrange for these persons to meet with the committee to brief it on its duties and on the plans of the association.

Printed materials on church planting may be obtained without charge from the missions offices of state conventions or from the Church Extension Division of the Home Mission Board. The committee should carefully study these how-to materials on church planting in order to develop its strategy. A study of the book *Planting New Churches,* by Jack Redford, would be helpful.

2. Selecting the Area of Need

The church missions committee should determine the area

where a new mission church needs to be planted. This should be done with the assistance of the associational missions director or the associational missions chairman. The associational leaders can pinpoint on a map where new churches are needed. They can guide the committee in identifying the areas of greatest need.

The committee should gather data about this location. From this research, the committee can come to a prayerful decision about the target group to be reached by the new unit. Some low income groups will remain permanent chapels. Other groups, with more adequate income, will become self-supporting.

3. Preparing the Church

The church missions committee should discuss plans for developing the local mission awareness of the church. It should bring to the church council a recommendation for plans particularly in cooperation with Brotherhood and WMU to educate the entire church as to the mission needs in the unchurched community. Also included should be plans for motivating church members to become involved in the project.

Once the mission awareness climate for local missions has been created, and the exact area of mission need has been pinpointed, data concerning the community should be presented to the congregation in the most effective way possible. Slide presentations could be shared in Brotherhood or Woman's Missionary Union meetings and with the entire church. Preaching by the pastor on missions is crucial to the success of total church involvement.

The climax of a church motivation plan would be to recommend that the church sponsor the new mission chapel. This should be a high spiritual moment in the church's life. A special time of prayer would be most appropriate.

After the church votes to sponsor the mission congregation, real preparation can begin. Church members who will be involved in the mission work must be trained in survey techniques, cultivative evangelism, leading home fellowship Bible classes, and neighborhood recreation programs. The Church Training program of the church may lead in the training to start the new work. The WMU and Brotherhood may have already conducted a mission action survey, which will give valuable information about the

125

community.

4. Cultivating the Mission Field

A community survey to locate unchurched people is the first action. Systematic, cultivative, get-acquainted visitation should follow the survey.

The church must begin making friends in the community where the new church is to be started. A helpful leaflet "Cultivating Community Events" may be secured from missions offices of state conventions or the Home Mission Board.

Mission action projects in the unchurched community conducted by the WMU or Brotherhood of the church will open doors and build an image of a church that cares.

5. Starting a Home Fellowship Mission

After relationships have been developed during the community cultivation period, a home fellowship mission should be started in a home or in several homes in the community. This may be an informal worship group, or it may be a Bible class using undated curriculum. Many materials describing the how-to of the fellowship are available from the state missions office, the Home Mission Board, or the Sunday School Board.

The church member in charge of the fellowship groups should be elected and trained by the sponsoring church. He should lead the group in visitation in the community, seeking to enlist the unchurched in the fellowship group. Ideally, at least four or five fellowship groups should be in operation before the mission chapel is formed. As the groups begin to respond, a rally of the fellowships can meet at some convenient place for corporate worship and planning toward the formal starting date of the mission chapel.

6. Organizing the Mission Chapel

The program of the mission chapel should be well-defined before its formal launching. The chapel might start with Sunday School and morning worship and continue to gather the congregation before launching other parts of a full church program.

A meeting place in or near the community must be secured.

Temporary facilities are usually found in banks, schools, motels, lodges, or other churches.

7. Financing the Venture

The handling of the offerings should be determined by the mother church. A mission budget should be planned and adopted. Regular financial reports should be given the mission congregation.

8. Planning a Building

While a site should be secured at an early date, building plans should be deferred until the congregation is ready to build on its own. The sponsoring church should assist the mission congregation in contacting and utilizing the resources of the Sunday School Board and the Home Mission Board in planning for facilities.

9. Constituting the Church

The formal organization of the mission congregation into a self-governing church should be delayed until the group is spiritually mature and stable enough to govern itself.

The church missions committee should make sure that the group is fully informed as to the mission of the church and its responsibilities for carrying out that mission in the world.

MISSIONS SUPPORT THROUGH CHRISTIAN STEWARDSHIP

The stewardship emphasis in a church should be designed to lead church members to become good stewards of their possessions. God is the owner of all things. God made the world and called it good (Gen. 1:1-31). He gave man dominion over his good world. God made man a steward or caretaker of the world.

The word *steward* shows the owner-manager relationship of God to man. In becoming the manager, man has the responsibility to take seriously the handling of the goods with which he is entrusted. The Christian steward seeks to fulfill God's purpose in his life in acquiring possessions, spending with a purpose, grow-

127

ing through giving, and planning for the future.

The responsibility of stewardship belongs to every Christian. Stewardship is not an option for the church, nor is it an elective for any Christian. Faithful and generous support of church ministries, including missions, is a privilege and duty that belongs to every believer. The support of missions is the genuine expression of the Christian life and the nature of the church. All resources should be viewed as a sacred trust from God. Thus, they are used to bring about his purpose on earth. The Christian steward gives all of life to Christ and seeks to honor God with his possessions.

A well-balanced stewardship emphasis in a church will develop Christian stewards and lead to increased support of world missions through the Cooperative Program.

1. Develop Christian Stewards

To develop Christian stewards is to seek to make clear the meaning of stewardship in the lives of church members. This also involves raising the level of individual and corporate giving to standards consistent with the ideals of biblical stewardship.

Each church must determine its purpose. In order to fulfill that purpose, each church has a responsibility to teach Christian stewardship. When a church teaches biblical stewardship, church members will be strengthened and the church's ministry at home and abroad will be enlarged.

The real meaning of stewardship is management. The word generally translated *steward* in the Bible relates to the management of the temporal affairs of another person.

Christian stewardship, then, encompasses more than giving. It is concerned with how a Christian relates to all material things, especially those over which he exercises some measure of control.

A Christian who recognizes that he is a manager of God's material world will see stewardship in a different light. Stewardship will include earning, spending, giving, and the final distribution of his possessions.

Earning.—A Christian steward will consider his method of earning as an exercise of his stewardship responsibility. He will honor God in his choice of vocation and in his performance on the job. He will view his job as one expression of his Christian commitment.

Spending.—Spending is another evidence of the depth of an individual's commitment to Christ. A Christian's earnings, no matter how small or great, are not his. They belong to God. Wasteful spending, spending for unworthy purposes, or the unwise use of credit indicates that a person does not understand fully his role as a Christian steward. A person who sees his income as a sacred trust seldom has difficulty moving up to the level of giving.

Giving.—Giving is the most visible stewardship activity. Giving as an expression of Christian stewardship rests on the foundation of earning and spending. When a person has committed his income in advance to debts, living expenses, and luxuries, his giving is unusually negligible.

Final distribution.—Final distribution of possessions is an important expression of Christian stewardship. Most families have estates of far greater value than they imagine. Some portions of the estate have increased in value since they were acquired. Real estate, insurance policies, stocks and bonds usually increase in worth over a period of years; but most people fail to consider this in their giving. A Christian's stewardship planning should include a means for allowing Christian causes to be included in the final distribution of his estate.

2. Support Cooperative Program Ministries

To support Cooperative Program ministries is to make church members aware of the Cooperative Program as the vital central plan for supporting their mission, educational, and benevolent undertakings. This support is channeled through their state convention and the Southern Baptist Convention.

Missions is at the heart of the church's life and work. A commitment to the financial support of missions is vital to the ministry of the church. The church should develop long-range plans for promoting all the ministries that are supported through the Cooperative Program.

The biblical basis for mission support should be taught in every phase of church life. Mission support information should be shared with all members. These teachings will increase their understanding of missions and call them to a greater commitment to the financial support of missions.

The persons who teach are church members who have been chosen and elected by the church for leadership positions in all the church organizations. The pastor will have responsibility for teaching stewardship and missions support through the Cooperative Program as a part of his ministry.

Persons are taught in ongoing situations and special emphases. They are taught in structured situations in large and small groups and in structured and unstructured situations as individuals. Teaching should take place during regular meetings of the church organizations, during the worship service, during the prayer service, and at special times.

Biblical stewardship, including the financial support of missions, may be taught anywhere. It may be taught in the church during meetings of church organizations and during worship services. It may be taught at special times in the church—during a week of Bible study, at a banquet, a money management conference, during Cooperative Program Day and Cooperative Program Month. It should be a continuous teaching effort all year.

To organize and carry out a stewardship emphasis, a church should utilize a church stewardship committee. The objective of the church stewardship committee is to communicate the biblical concepts of individual and corporate stewardship. The committee will utilize all functions of the church to accomplish its objective. The committee consists of a chairman and four or more sections. These sections are stewardship education, mission, budget, and accounting.

All church organizations should assist in communicating stewardship information. All stewardship activities should be coordinated with other church activities through the church council and placed on the church calendar.

---

1. This quotation is from the *Good News Bible,* the Bible in Today's English Version. Old Testament: Copyright © American Bible Society 1976; New Testament: Copyright © American Bible Society 1966, 1971, 1976. Used by permission. Subsequent quotations are marked GNB.

Chapter 10

Building an Effective Music Ministry

A church's music ministry is a complex and unique program of many experiences and activities. It includes the music experiences of congregational services, church music performance groups, music activity groups, music study groups, and individual musicians. In all these the church family involves itself in music experiences appropriate to the needs of individuals of all ages to help accomplish the mission of the church.

The music educational experiences are intended to develop musical skill, attitudes, and understandings of persons. These experiences evolve in many ways and are related to the total educational thrust of the church. But the music ministry is more than educational experience.

THE MUSIC MINISTRY IN THE CHURCH

The music experiences of the congregational services are a vital part of the church's life. Great congregational singing can be an exciting experience for the church family. The vibrant singing of the gathered congregation joining in songs of praise and testimony can do much to enhance the spirit of the church.

1. The Apostle Paul's Admonitions

To the church in Corinth, Paul the apostle wrote, "I will sing with the spirit, and I will sing with the understanding also" (1 Cor. 14:15). Paul is saying that the singing should be Spirit-filled and that the singing should be understood by the singer. Singing is a spiritual experience; it should be understood by the singer. If there is no understanding, the singing has no meaning. Christian song is the overflow of the Christian heart. If the heart is full, the singing will also be full. In his book *The Hymnody of the Christian Church,* Louis F. Benson refers to Christian song as a spiritual gift which each Christian brings to the sanctuary and contributes to a common song of spiritual fellowship.

To the church at Colossae, Paul wrote, "Let the word of Christ dwell in you richly in all wisdom; teaching and admonishing one another in psalms and hymns and spiritual songs, singing with grace in your hearts to the Lord. And whatsoever ye do in word or deed, do all in the name of the Lord Jesus, giving thanks to God and the Father by him" (Col. 3:16-17). This passage outlines the direction, the dimension, the declaration, and the desirability of the church's music ministry.

2. The Music Director

The church family looks to the music director for strong leadership, whether he is a full-time staff person, a part-time staff person, or one who gives leadership as a volunteer. Whether the person is called a minister of music, a music director, or a congregational song leader, he has opportunities for expressing judgment about the music experiences made, shared, or listened to by the congregation. He must choose carefully the hymns and choir music. He should not rely only on his own musical taste. His judgment in administrative leadership must reflect the broad spectrum of tastes of the congregation as he ministers to their needs through music.

3. The Organist and the Pianist

While instrumental groups may be used frequently or infrequently in the church, the major responsibility for providing supportive accompaniment for congregational singing, choral music by the choirs, and solo musicians is borne by the organist and the pianist. Skillful playing of these keyboard instruments by persons who understand the appropriate roles of the organ and piano within the church service can add much to the spirit of the services.

4. Congregational Hymn Singing

When the church body gathers for worship, the hymn singing is done by the congregation—all the people together. This unstructured, ungraded, unorganized body of people, all ages together, made up of some eager singers, some reluctant singers, and some nonsingers, is a group that is involved in "making the music" of hymn singing. Singing together is only one of several possible experiences within the framework of the congregational service that the people do for themselves. If the hymn singing is great and expressive, it is because the people make it so. The music leader cannot produce great singing by himself. The choir cannot make up for a lack of participation by the congregation. At the time of congregational singing, the choir becomes a part of the congregation, rather than a group set apart from the rest of the people.

5. Music Groups

During the congregational services there are opportunities for individuals to participate in music groups to provide musical experiences in which the rest of the people are listeners. These groups are usually organized on an age basis—preschool, children, youth, adult. These opportunities not only involve participation in music performance but also focus upon the musical and spiritual development of the individual. (In this discussion the use of the word *performance* is intended to mean "the doing of it," rather than a "show, a concert, or a presentation.")

Unquestioned musical standards—singing or playing in tune, with careful balance and blend, with careful attention to diction of the singers, with awareness of the musical phrase, dynamic levels, and interpretative meaning—are not to be compromised in the church.

The performances of these groups within the congregational service may serve a priestly or prophetic function. In the priestly role, the choir expresses praise, petition, and confession to God on behalf of the congregation. The choir sings music that the congregation cannot sing for itself. In a similar manner, one person voices a prayer in the service, leading the prayer, or praying on behalf of all the persons present in the service. This is the priestly role of the choir singing a text addressed by God.

In the prophetic role, the choir may exhort, teach, instruct, warn, or otherwise prophesy to the congregation on behalf of God—singing God's message through scriptural texts or doctrinal truths poetically expressed. In this role the choir speaks to the congregation through the song in the same manner that the preacher speaks to the congregation on behalf of the Lord—the preaching of God's message to God's people.

Usually the major responsibility for the music of the congregational service is given to the adult and youth groups. The frequency of service performance has a high potential with these two age groups. This responsibility for weekly performance places a great significance on the weekly rehearsal schedules. Because of the spiritual, esthetic, and emotional—as well as musical—values involved, rehearsals bring a warmth and togetherness to a choir that does not always exist in other groups or classes in the church structure. The need to make the best possible preparation for a team effort in the congregational services on the next Lord's Day is a matter of keen awareness to all those in the choir.

In these instrumental and choral groups, performance is a high priority—singing together for the glory of God. The choir works on the right words, the right notes, and the right rhythm. Sloppy, mediocre, careless singing is an abomination to the Lord; it should be studiously avoided in God's house.

At the same time, the musical and vocal development of the individual goes on. Across weeks and weeks of regular participation in the group, the individual should improve as a singer, as a music reader, as a member of the team.

Preschoolers.—The music experiences which the church provides for preschoolers and children (grades 1 to 6) are largely educational in purpose. The children's groups will have some opportunities to make a musical contribution to the congregational services—especially the older children (grades 4, 5, 6). Seldom will preschoolers be involved in congregational services.

Music is a vibrant, vital source of experience through which preschoolers learn about God, Jesus, the natural world, themselves, and others. All preschoolers enjoy music in some form when they come to their church, but only four's and five's take part in an organized program of musical experiences.

Music can contribute a great deal to the spiritual development of preschoolers. Songs about God, Jesus, Bible, church, family, self, others, and the natural world help preschoolers form concepts related to Bible truths. Music helps preschoolers experience wonder and joy in a wonderful way. Preschoolers may experience feelings of well-being and personal worth as they sing and are accepted by others. Preschoolers become sensitive to the beauty of music. Music provides opportunities for relaxation and rhythmic response. Music is a medium through which preschoolers find outlets for emotions. Preschoolers may be creative as they make their own tunes, words, or rhythms.

Children.—As a child develops and grows through the first six grades of elementary education, music provided in the life of the church takes on increasing significance. For the child, music is a source of enjoyment. It gives him an opportunity to participate in activities that let him sing, move, listen, or create, as he wishes. Music helps bring about the expression of self as music activities—singing, playing instruments, moving, listening—allow each child to find his or her own expression. Music brings enrichment to the daily routine as natural musical responses can be channeled toward meaningful results.

Musical experiences aid concept development—spiritual concepts, musical concepts, and other concepts about self, the world, science, health, family, and friends—as these emerge in the mind and understanding of the child. Music enriches the social and emotional lives of children in this significant area of their growth.

Youth.—Youth is a wonderful age—a time of discovery, learning, experimentation. Musical growth heightens the ability of youth to understand and grasp. Physical development brings a maturity to the singing voice, and the boy sopranos and altos become sturdy tenors and basses. The thrill of sharing in ensemble singing—in voice parts, two, three, four, or more—brings musical excitement unknown in earlier ages. Greater frequency of performance is now possible. Choir retreats and choir tours are new areas of keen interest involving musical, social, witnessing, and mission endeavors that build strong morale. The achievement of excellent performance brings a sense of inner warmth felt only by those who have paid the price in rehearsal, determination, and discipline. The spiritual values of these musical experiences enriches young lives and deepens their spiritual sensitivity. Many youth are brought to a knowledge of the Savior through music participation.

Adults.—From eighteen or eighty and past is a joyful lifetime of abundant experiences in music in the life of the church. An adult can find satisfying involvement and expression in music activity in many ways—singing, playing, sharing, listening, helping others to enjoy great sounds of music. Unique opportunities exist for music involvement by special adult groups—single adults, singles again, and senior adults.

6. Music in the Other Church Programs

In the other structures of church life—Sunday School, Church Training, Woman's Missionary Union, and Brotherhood—the sounds of music are woven tightly into the fabric of their activities. Songs appropriate to each age level are usually part of the total experience at each meeting of these groups. Songs and hymns help reaffirm biblical truths and doctrinal beliefs. Songs and hymns appropriate to the dated curriculum help to reenforce the truths contained in the lesson materials.

Excellent opportunities are afforded for the use of musical talent in department activities. Song leaders and pianists, as well as individuals, ensembles, and groups providing special music, can provide music leadership in these departments. Playing the piano in Sunday School or Church Training can afford excellent opportunities for young pianists and young people with potential keyboard ability to develop their musical skills.

The hymn singing of these departments can be related effectively to the hymn singing of the congregational services. In department and group meetings new hymns can be learned that will increase participation in the congregational services. The departmental leader is actually leading a segment of the congregation. He can bring helpful music emphases to increase participation in the church services.

THE WORK OF THE MUSIC MINISTRY

The work of the music ministry in the church is best expressed through its task statements. Tasks are basic continuing activities of primary importance to a program in helping to move

136

the church on its mission. Through the following tasks the work of the music ministry is accomplished.

Task 1: Provide Musical Experiences in Congregational Services

This task assigns to the music ministry the responsibility of planning, rehearsing, arranging, performing, and leading music for the congregational services. The music ministry is given the responsibility of making available the musical resources that are needed to help achieve the purpose of congregational services. The congregational services include any corporate gathering of a local church congregation for worship, witness, proclamation, nurture, ministry, or fellowship.

In suggesting a formula for a healthy, growing church, Peter Wagner, church growth specialist, stresses the need for celebration in the worship experience. In his book *Your Church Can Grow,* he urges a festival kind of worship experience. He points out that vibrant, effective music and singing can set a tone for a church and make other people want to attend and join the celebration.

Essential actions.—This task involves the following essential actions of those who lead the music ministry:

• Assist the pastor in planning the congregational services.
• Lead in selecting, rehearsing, arranging, and performing music for congregational services.
• Lead the congregation in relevant, meaningful, inspiring musical experiences that contribute to the thrust and mission of the church.
• Motivate the church constituency to want to be involved in the musical experiences and to grow in their understanding of the role of music in the congregational services.
• Provide resources for musical experiences of the congregation.
• Assist church organizations in enlisting and training song leaders and accompanists for their departmental and organizational meetings.

Task 2: Develop Musical Skills, Attitudes, and Understanding

To achieve this task, the leaders of the music ministry will plan and carry out a definite schedule of teaching, training and performance activities to develop positive attitudes toward church music, increase understandings of the full dimension of church music, and guide persons in developmental learning and performance experiences.

The skills of music involve learning to read music notation. Special skills are also involved in singing and playing music. Attitudes and understandings are developed as one becomes aware of the historical development of music, the individuals who have contributed to our music literature, and the appropriate use of music in the life of the church and its people.

The music ministry should involve church members and prospects in responsible discipleship which results in the use of their talents in the worship and service of the church. New members are easily assimilated into the fellowship of the church through involvement in music activities. Through music experiences persons are led to a lifelong commitment to Jesus Christ and responsible church membership.

Christian children, youth, and adults need to understand that they are part of the fellowship of believers—the body of Christ. As members of the body, all Christian disciples have unique functions to fulfill. The music ministry is engaged in helping members discover their musical talents, develop those talents to the fullest potential, and use their musical abilities to God's glory. As talents are developed and exercised, the spirit of the church is freshened and the tempo of church growth is quickened.

Resources.—This task is implemented through a curriculum with balanced approach to music education and music performance. This material involves sequential and progressive learning and performance activities based on mental, physical, and spiritual readiness of individuals. This task leads participants in the music ministry to make use of their musical skills through structured educational and performance activities that result in personal development, Christian growth, and the use of talents to support the mission of the church. The curriculum is contained in leader and member age-graded periodicals, Church Study Course materials, and related products.

Essential actions.—This task involves the following essential actions of the music ministry:

138

- Discover and analyze music teaching, training, and performance needs of the church constituency.
- Provide the church constituency appropriate music learning, training, and performance opportunities.
- Lead the church constituency to be involved in music learning, training, and performance activities.

Task 3: Witness and Minister Through Music

This task assigns to the music ministry the responsibility of leading persons to witness and minister through music experiences and activities in the church and the community. The music ministry will seek ways to witness through music to believers and unbelievers and to use the music resources of the church in ministering to the human and spiritual needs of church members.

The successful implementation of this task will lead to church growth. Emphasizing the priorities necessary for effective evangelism, McGavran and Arn point out that "churches grow when priority is given to effective evangelism, which includes proclamation and persuasion."[1] Effectiveness is improved when Christ is proclaimed in the "heart language" of the people involved. The music ministry has a unique opportunity to witness to God's love through the "heart language" of gospel music.

In his book on church growth, C. B. Hogue of the Home Mission Board further describes the place of the music ministry in witnessing:

"Church Music has, in fact, a strong opportunity for witness because it gives individuals a chance to personally express the joy and hope of their faith in a manner that does not seem blatant or offensive. Music obviously enhances congregational worship. It provides a dynamic emotional outlet for personal witness. It offers a warm, sensitive atmosphere in which individuals can make conversion decision, and it can give depth and life to what might otherwise be a cold and unfeeling experience.

"But this is only the traditional aspect of the Church Music program. Today's skilled choirs have opportunities to sing on television, in shopping centers, at festivals, and fairs. In such places, their contemporary sound can testify to their biblical faith. Their witness can be as forceful as it is entertaining. The Southern Baptist Convention, for example, uses hundreds of choir tour groups each summer in its mission outreach efforts. Estimates are that these groups sing before thousands of non-Christians each year, many of whom would have no other exposure to the gospel message. The number of persons who have made commitments to Christ as a result of these performances can only be guessed, but Southern Baptist leaders believe they contribute significantly to the denomination's continued and outstanding church growth during the past ten years."[2]

Wendell Belew feels that other churches need to rediscover the early tools of the church: music and drama. He urges that the music program "be adapted to attract those who are outside (the church) and who may not have the same level of appreciation."[3] He cites an example of one church that registered 130 decisions for Christ as the result of a music program in a shopping center, followed by personal counseling and sharing of testimonies.

Content and materials.—The music ministry will involve its members in proclaiming the good news of God in Jesus Christ and giving themselves in unselfish service to others. Most of the actions involve musical proclamation and witness or providing comfort, solace, encouragement, affirmation, or support. Sometimes these actions may not be expressed through music. They will provide for the physical needs of those who need this concern.

The music content for this task may range from simple songs to major musical performances—song sermons, cantatas, musicals, and musical dramas. The type of music will depend on the nature of the opportunity and the needs of those to be reached.

Essential actions.—This task involves the following essential actions of the music ministry:

 • Discover and analyze needs for musical witness and ministry.
 • Develop plans for individual and group involvement in musical witness and ministry.
 • Involve members in individual and group musical witness and ministry projects.

Task 4: Provide and Interpret Information Concerning the Work of the Church and the Denomination

Church members need to know the emphasis of the church and denominational program. This task places on the music ministry and other church programs the responsibility for sharing this information.

To provide means to take the initiative in gathering and distributing the information. *To interpret* indicates the necessity of explaining or presenting the information in such a way that the intended message can be responded to in an appropriate manner. Information includes news, data, emphasis, activities, or other factual material. Incorporated in the term *work* are the activities of the church or groups with which the church cooperates to perform its mission locally and around the world.

It is important that Southern Baptists work together toward worthy objectives. Coordination and cooperation are possible only when the lines of communication are kept open between church members and denominational leaders.

Content.—This material deals with the activities of the church and the denominational at the local level, in the association, in the state convention, and in the Southern Baptist Convention. It is the task of all church programs and services.

The music heard in the churches has experienced as much change in recent years as any area of the church's life. To see the shifting tides of church music is an exciting experience. To be caught up in this action can be quite breathtaking. However strange and unsettling the signs and sounds may be to those who don't like change, we need to understand that this is not the first time such events have occurred in Christian song. Neither will it be the last. To be able to harness the vitality and strength of church music in this day and to use it in the church's mission, boldly and skillfully, is a challenge that demands our best.

Christian song is dynamic, everchanging, because God made man a curious, restless being, and because God's revelation of himself is an everunfolding experience. Restless man knows more about God's world and God's universe today than ever before. Our worship should be more significant, our praise more glorious, our witness more genuine, and our proclamation of the gospel more effective than it has ever been.

Baptist churches are autonomous. There is great diversity of musical taste among these churches. This means there will never be a uniform, precise music ministry that will fit every church. All that has been said here must be adapted, shaped, rearranged, and altered to meet the needs of the individual church. Music leaders, under the guidance of the Holy Spirit, will find ways within the broad guidelines provided to use effectively the talents and resources they have available.

God in his Word exhorts us to praise him, to "come before his presence with singing." In his church, in all its activities, music is a vital experience. It voices praise, it testifies to the power of the gospel for salvation, it bears witness to the vitality of the Christian life. It reaches the unreached, it goes beyond closed doors, it communicates Christian love and understanding, it calms and heals and comforts. Those who have leadership responsibility in all areas of church life will wisely seek ways to use musical resources to help the church achieve its mission.

---

1. Donald A. McGavran and Winfield C. Arn, *Ten Steps for Church Growth* (New York: Harper and Row, 1977), p. 53.
2. C. B. Hogue, *I Want My Church to Grow* (Nashville: Broadman Press, 1977), p. 95.
3. M. Wendell Belew, *Churches and How They Grow* (Nashville: Broadman Press, 1971), pp. 56-57.

Chapter 11

Providing Support Through Service Programs

During the eighties society will grow increasingly complex and specialized. People in decision-making positions will have to learn to call on experts in specialized fields to help them sort through various alternatives and name the right choices. Service institutions that provide specialized consultation, information, and resources to these decision-makers will come into their own.

Churches will also have a need for specialized consultation. They will come to depend more and more on consultation and support services within their own structure. These services exist to help the church operate and conduct its ministry more effectively.

The three service programs in a church are media services, recreation services, and administrative services.

MEDIA SERVICES

The eighties offer unlimited potential for new and expanded dimensions in church media services. In the contemporary age with its emphasis on mass communication, and especially electronic communication, churches must use a wide variety of media in their programs.

Educators point out the absolute necessity of an extensive collection of media and a far-reaching program of media services. Churches must also see media services as vital to an active, forceful program of outreach and education.

In her book *The School Library Media Center*, Ruth Ann Davies defines media as "carriers of knowledge."[1] These carriers of knowledge must be made available to church leaders and members to assist them in implementing their tasks as Christians. Media refers to the materials provided by the media services staff and housed in the church media center. Included are: (1) printed

143

materials (books, periodicals, newspapers, tracts, leaflets, and clippings from newspapers or magazines); (2) projected visuals and audiovisuals (slides, filmstrips, overhead transparencies, motion pictures, video cassettes, video discs, and microfiche); (3) audio materials (disc recordings and tape recordings); (4) audiovisual equipment (8mm, 16mm, and 35mm projectors, opaque projectors, overhead projectors, tape recorders, record players, cassette duplicators, video recorders and players, video monitors, portable public address systems, and microfiche readers); (5) nonprojected visuals (maps, charts, flipcharts, sentence-strip charts, posters, flat pictures, framed art pieces, games, and globes); (6) other miscellaneous materials (multimedia kits, costumes, permanent flower arrangements, "props" for drama groups, and objects); and (7) music resources (as requested by the music ministry).

The task of the church media services program is to educate persons in the use of media and provide media and media services to support the church in the achievement of its mission. An examination of this task statement reveals the impact which an effective media services program can have in a church.

1. Educate Persons in the Use of Media

Church leaders and members often need guidance in understanding the value of media in their personal lives and in their church-related activities. They need to know the specific titles and types of media available and how to use those media effectively. These persons need to be led to see media as tools that can be valuable to them in learning, growing, teaching, ministering, and witnessing.

The media services staff performs this educational function in many ways. Individual conferences, special workshops, and presentations in regularly scheduled meetings offer opportunities for media education. Promotional avenues such as posters, bulletin boards, displays, announcements, skits, and other visual and oral means may also be used to inform church members and leaders of media and their use.

Media education may take place in the media center, in other locations in the church building, or even in the homes of church members. This education may occur at any time—on a scheduled basis or spontaneously. The media services staff should try to establish an on-going program of media education to keep members and leaders updated and informed about materials and services and their optimum use.

2. Provide Media and Media Services to Support the Church in the Achievement of Its Mission

Because of the extensive number of media, the expense of materials and equipment, and the complexity of the media field, it would be impossible for each church leader and member to provide for himself all the items and equipment needed for effective teaching, learning, and growing. For the same reasons, units of church programs would find it impractical to provide the materials needed by leaders and participants. In addition, efforts to furnish titles in program units restrict the number of items available as well as adding unnecessary additional costs. Therefore, it is logical that a church provide media and media services through the media services staff and the media center.

Along with providing media, the media services personnel is involved in media services. A media service may be defined as a group of actions which encourage the use of media in special ministries, in personal study, in teaching and training, and in reaching people.

In providing media, the media services staff: (1) selects those items to meet the total needs of the church people and programs; (2) secures the media from stores and agencies; (3) processes, catalogs, and stores media; and (4) circulates media by lending, selling, or giving. This providing involves a number of persons and much time and effort on the part of media workers.

As a part of providing media services, the media staff tries to identify opportunities and needs for such services. They work with church and program leaders to establish systems for the service and to secure space, money, and personnel. The staff is then given the responsibility of instituting, maintaining, and refining the service. An example of a media service would be the beginning of a tract distribution plan. The media services staff would investigate the possibility of the plan and follow through to its initiation and operation. In each church the alert media services staff will recognize the need for many such services.

145

3. Effects of Dynamic Church Media Services

The incorporation of media into church programs and activities can give an added dimension to these programs. Media can stimulate new interest, maintain attention, and generate better learning. While basic quarterlies and texts provide core information and speakers and leaders can convey certain facts and ideas by the spoken word, media can bring a sense of feeling and emotion to certain studies. Here are three examples of the value of effective media services.

In Bible study.—In studying a Bible section such as one of the journeys of Paul, the use of a motion picture can help the viewer identify with Paul in his opportunities, problems, and situations. The viewer is able to have a better understanding of the Scripture passage as he sees the land where Paul ministered, the modes of travel, and even his clothing and living conditions.

In missions education.—The program of missions education is enhanced by the use of such media as pictures, films and filmstrips, maps, recorded experiences of missionaries, and biographies of missionaries. Children, especially, have an enlarged vision of the world and the needs of its people through media that is used effectively.

In outreach.—Another example of the use of media involves the witnessing and outreach programs of the church. Visitors may distribute attractive tracts which present the plan of salvation or which relate to specific needs or questions of persons. Visitors may also secure from the media center certain materials which speak to the special interests or problems of the persons to whom they are witnessing.

Suppose a church member is trying to reach a family with a handicapped child. The visitor, in discussing this situation with a member of the media services staff, is guided to a book about a family or child with a similar problem. In taking the book to the family, the visitor is able to show his concern in a tangible way. He can leave the book with the family. He has reason to return later to retrieve the book and talk further with the family. His act can be a means of expressing genuine support to the family, and it can continue over an indefinite period. Since he established a relationship of caring and concern, the visitor's efforts to witness are often more readily received.

During the eighties the church must use every possible means to help its leaders and members reach people for Christ and develop and strengthen Christians. An active media services program can support the church in achieving its mission.

RECREATION SERVICES

During the eighties people will have more leisure time than ever before. Christians need to be taught the value of leisure and conservative recreational activities. More and more churches are discovering the value of an active recreation program. An effective recreation ministry begins with a Christian view of leisure.

1. Leisure and the Christian

"To every thing there is a season, and a time to every purpose under the heaven" (Eccl. 3:1).

All of man's time is a gift from God. Time is a medium of human existence, a frame of reference, created by God. All of the Christian's lifetime is given as a gift. Recognition of this fact should make the Christian realize that neither work nor leisure is to be endured or wasted.

Leisure is defined as a block of unoccupied time when one is free to do what he chooses. Leisuretime is time beyond that required for existence, the things which we must do biologically to stay alive (eat, sleep, eliminate, etc.). Leisure is also time beyond that required for subsistence, the things we must do to make a living (work, school preparation, etc.).

The Christian view of leisure is two-dimensional: quantitative and qualitative. The quantitative view deals with cyclic time, rhythmic time, chronologic time, natural time, historic time, free time, work time, study time, and so forth. The qualitative view adds the choice of opportunity—what one chooses to do with his time. There is much truth in the saying, "What a person is depends upon what he does when he has nothing to do." Free choice of leisure pursuit reveals the deeper self.

One frame of reference involving the consumption of leisure is recreation. Recreation takes place during leisure. Recreation is

147

activity designed to create, to restore, and to refresh the individual. Recreation is both serious and purposeful. It is an avenue of living which should lead to fuller discovery of self.

2. Task of Recreation Services

The task of recreation services in a church is to provide recreation methods, materials, services, and experiences that will enrich the lives of persons and support the total mission of the church.

Recreation plays a positive role in helping a church do its work. It can be a direct role as the work of the church is expressed in recreation activities themselves. By providing ideas, equipment and methods for use by other church programs, recreation takes on the role of service and support. A church which recognizing its responsibility to the whole person—physical, social, mental, and spiritual—will include in its program a ministry of recreation to help meet these needs.

3. Purpose and Place

Recreation services will achieve its purpose as a channel of service and support, a catalyst in outreach, a vehicle for ministry and mission action, a tool for teaching, an environment for fellowship, and an avenue to abundant living.

As a channel of service and support, recreation complements, undergirds, and strengthens Bible teaching by becoming a workshop in everyday Christian living. It also extends Bible study through camp and retreat settings. It can be mission action taking the form of recreation. It can also be a dynamic of worship and proclamation as dramatic presentations are used to enhance communication of the message.

Recreation becomes a catalyst in outreach when recreation activities are used to proclaim the gospel. It is also a catalyst in outreach when recreation activities are sponsored to reach those persons for whom recreation is the most effective means of encounter with Christ. Recreation provides a setting for cultivating the unreached and enlisting them in other church activities where the gospel will be proclaimed.

Recreation becomes a vehicle for ministry when recreational

skills are applied to meet needs where natural disaster or tragedy has occurred. Recreation can also be used in a therapeutic role to help the ill, the deaf, the blind, the crippled, and the mentally retarded. It is also a ministry when applied to the needs of the aging, when used to bring joy and new hope to the under-privileged, and when used by the missionary to extend Christian compassion, service, and witness around the world.

Recreation is a tool for teaching when used to establish a climate conducive to learning, or when viewed as a workshop in daily living. It is also a teaching laboratory as it provides creative methods for communicating Christian principles.

As an environment for fellowship, recreation supports the life of the church in the development of koinonia. It provides experiences to help Christians realize anew that they belong to God and to one another.

Recreation becomes an avenue to abundant living as it opens the door to a whole new way of life. It provides new opportunities, challenges, and choices in the Christian's leisure. Recreation becomes a positive force in shaping personality and character as it calls for high ethical and moral standards. Through its vast resource of activities and experiences, it provides joy, fun, relaxation, fellowship, release, and restoration for church members.

4. Areas of Recreation Programming

Social recreation.—Social recreation is activity engaged in during one's leisuretime that involves interaction of people with people. Social recreation is usually expressed as parties, banquets, fellowships, picnics, or other similar activities.

Social recreation is people having fun. Social recreation is a place for meeting new people. Social recreation is an opportunity to strengthen already established relationships. Social recreation represents an opportunity for the individual to grow socially.

Social recreation strengthens relationships within a church, building the *koinonia*—the fellowship of believers in Christ. The *koinonia* of a church is enriched by people worshiping together, singing together, praying together, experiencing joy or pain or sorrow together, and by playing and laughing together.

Social recreation is vital in outreach to those beyond the

church, to those whom the church is seeking to reach for Christ.

Social recreation will help strengthen church-community relationships. It can help build good relationships with other churches in the community.

Sports and games.—Sports and games include physical or mental games or contests where teams or individuals place their skills and abilities in opposition to their opponents. The purpose of sports and games is competition and enjoyment, fellowship with others, and physical exercise. Christ-centered sports programs will include opportunities for the individual to give or receive a positive Christian witness, and to develop the personal qualities of honesty, dependability, patience, self-control, perseverance, courage, responsibility, sportsmanship, and teamwork.

Sports activities in the local church include team sports such as soccer, flag football, softball, baseball, basketball, and volleyball; lifetime sports such as archery, bicycling, boating or sailing, golf, and hiking; individual sports such as riflery, hunting and fishing, gymnastics, skating, skiing, bowling, and horseback riding; and dual sports such as tennis, badminton, horseshoes, table tennis, handball or racketball, and croquet.

Drama.—Church drama portrays the Christian life and the conflict of forces in life from the Christian perspective. It is also used often to explore a person's relationship to God, to his fellowman, and to himself.

Drama permits the Christian to witness not only through voice, emotions, and daily life-style but also through his total being. The Christian's body, when imaginatively projected into character, dialogue, and action, becomes a vibrant, powerful force for witnessing.

The major forms of church drama include storytelling, puppetry, monologue, improvisation, creative dramatics, choral drama, pantomime, tableau, music drama, play production, fun drama, readers theater, and multimedia.

Camping.—Church camping is camping that utilizes the resources of the natural environment for Christian education, fellowship, evangelism, ministry, and personal growth. It also uses the creation to teach about the Creator.

Church camping helps fulfill the spiritual and physical needs of individuals, both Christian and non-Christian. This helps the church reach its objectives. These objectives are to win the lost to Christ and to guide persons in a progressive development toward Christian maturity.

Forms of church camping are retreat camping, travel camping, day camping, resident camping, wilderness camping, backpacking, primitive or pioneer camping, Christian stress camping, and family camping.

Recreation music.—Recreation music is that music, vocal or instrumental, used in a recreation setting. It is music used by an individual or a group for pure fun and enjoyment and for fellowship and worship. It is hard to think of a social activity—banquet, party, or fellowship—without some music. And can you imagine a camping or retreat experience without music?

Retreats.—Retreat is a time and place for church members to disengage from the mundane and the routines of life. Retreat is a time to lay aside thoughts of business and personal care, not because they have no rightful demand upon us, but because we permit them to consume too much of life. Retreat is a time of solitude and introspection, a time to think, to pray, to talk, and to listen.

Retreats may be classified into four broad categories: church leadership, age-group, organizational, and special emphasis.

Arts, crafts, and hobbies.—Arts, crafts, and hobbies may be defined as an individual's use of his hands to create, to form an expression of the culture of the moment. In so doing he expresses something of his own personality and experiences self-satisfaction and enjoyment. He also creates enjoyment for others who see that creation.

Physical fitness.—A church should encourage its members to take care of their physical bodies. It can do this by providing guidance and program suggestions to help them achieve and maintain good health and fitness.

Physical fitness can be defined as good health. Good health and fitness don't happen automatically. These must be developed and maintained by the individual on a regular, ongoing basis. Physical fitness is a program of regular conditioning of the mind and body.

Physical fitness is a measure of the body's strength, stamina, and flexibility. It is the ability to perform daily work effectively without undue fatigue, to survive unexpected physical emergencies, and to have sufficient energy remaining to enjoy the recreational pursuits of leisure. In the psychological sense, physical fitness relates to how one looks and feels—mentally, emotionally, and physically.

Therapeutic recreation.—Leisure ministries to persons of special need—the blind, deaf, retarded, emotionally maladjusted, crippled, and otherwise handicapped—should be included in a church recreation program. Recreation can make a real contribution to these ministries.

The church on mission in the eighties should put high priority on all aspects of recreation because of the dynamic thrust it affords to both the individual and the church for Bold Mission Thrust. The recreation ministry is committed to helping the church reach its mission.

ADMINISTRATIVE SERVICES

A Baptist church gathered is its own governing body. It alone is responsible for all of its administrative work. But the church assembled cannot attend to all its administrative needs. A church can work more effectively if it limits its work to decision making and delegates to officers and committees the responsibility to study, plan, and recommend procedures and solutions to administrative problems.

All church officers and committees share the common task of assisting the church to plan its program, manage its resources, and govern its life and work. The duties of each officer and committee grow out of and are a breakdown of this general task. The following definition will give a better understanding of the meaning of this task.

Assist means to give support or aid. The implication is that this task describes how the church goes about making decisions in planning, managing, and governing. Administrative services do not make these decisions through studies and recommendations. Administrative services, upon request or assignment, may administer operational activities for the church.

Plan means to determine a mode of operation and a course of action.

Manage is to direct or carry on the business affairs of the church as requested or assigned to support mission and programs.

Govern refers to guiding and directing. Governing is the means by which a church regulates or rules. The implication is that the church gathered is ultimately responsible for the control of its affairs. Administrative services are means by which the church gathered assists the church in guiding and directing the affairs of the church. These administrative services are performed by groups or persons who report to the church assembled.

Life and work of the church refers to the spiritual and physical operation of the church.

1. Duties of Church Committees

Churches have many committees that do their administrative work. Here are the duties of some committees that many churches have.

(1) Evangelism Committee
   a. Consult with and assist the pastor to develop and present to the church council an aggressive and perennial program of evangelism.
   b. Evaluate the response of the church to its evangelistic opportunities.
   c. Seek to develop among church members a spiritual awakening which is conducive to evangelism.
   d. Work with church program organizations to enlist and equip lay persons to become effective witnesses for Christ.
   e. Request, through proper channels, adequate personnel, calendar time and finances to implement church goals and action plans assigned to the evangelism committee.
   f. Work with the Sunday School to establish and maintain up-to-date files on non-Christian prospects.

(2) Nominating Committee
   a. Select, interview, and enlist church program leaders, church committee chairmen, and general church officers.
   b. Approve volunteer workers before they are invited to service in church-elected leadership positions.
   c. Distribute church leadership according to priority needs.

153

      d. Assist church leaders to discover and enlist qualified persons to fill church-elected positions of leadership in their respective organizations.

      e. Present volunteer workers to the church for election.

      f. Nominate special committees as assigned by the church.

(3) Church Property and Space Committee

      a. Inspect all church properties periodically and maintain inventory.

      b. Conduct with program leaders an annual evaluation of space allocations to determine areas needing adjustment and enlargement.

      c. Recommend space rearrangement to secure maximum use for education, special activity, and worship; seek new space as needed (rent or borrow) to provide for continued growth.

      d. Work with church missions committee to recommend acquisition and to maintain property and space for mission purposes.

      e. Recommend to the personnel committee the employment training needs and supervision needs of maintenance personnel.

      f. Develop and recommend maintenance policies and procedures.

      g. Recommend policies regarding the use of space, equipment, and properties.

      h. Develop and recommend an adequate insurance plan to protect all buildings and properties.

      i. Prepare recommendations for the stewardship committee and administer the budget regarding maintenance of all property.

      j. Assist the church in arranging, equipping, and administering adequate worship space.

      k. Assist the church in determining, acquiring, and administering parking space.

      l. Assist the church in selecting and maintaining proper and adequate furnishings for the church programs and activities.

      m. Assist other church committees in responsibilities relating to church property and space.

n. Recommend to the church the appointment of a church building survey and planning committee when needed and appropriate.

o. Promote the conservation of energy and other natural resources used in the operation of church facilities.

(4) Stewardship Committee
   a. Develop and recommend to the church council an overall stewardship information plan.
   b. Develop and recommend to the church a budget.
   c. Plan and direct the church's budget subscription plan.
   d. Conduct studies and make recommendations to the church concerning proposed expenditures not included in the budget.
   e. Review expenditures periodically in terms of budget allocations and budget adjustments to the church.
   f. Develop and recommend to the church financial policies and procedures.

(5) Family Life Committee
   a. Survey family life needs.
   b. Develop and recommend to the church council an overall family life plan.
   c. Plan and direct various family life projects.
   d. Lead the church to develop a ministry to singles, senior adults, and intergenerational groups as needed.
   e. Coordinate plans and activities through the church council.

(6) Flower Committee
   a. Recommend policies and procedures for securing, arranging, and disposing of flowers for congregational services.
   b. Recommend policies related to providing flowers for sick and bereaved members.
   c. Work with budget section of the stewardship committee in requesting flower committee budget.
   d. Secure, place, and dispose of flower arrangements.

(7) Food Services Committee
   a. Consult with church leaders to determine the food service needs of the church.

b. Recommend to the church the food services to be provided.

c. Develop and recommend policies and procedures for the church's food services.

d. Communicate approved food service policies and procedures to the church membership.

e. Recommend to the personnel committee the employment, training, and supervision of food service personnel.

f. Evaluate food services and report on the efficiency to the church.

(8) History Committee

a. Gather and preserve all church records of the past.

b. Assist in recording of present-day activities.

c. Use historical facts and documents to challenge the church to accomplish its mission.

d. Develop and recommend to the church policies and procedures regarding its historical materials.

(9) Missions Committee

a. Conduct studies and recommend plans for local mission work.

b. Work through the church council to coordinate the mission work of the church.

c. Request and administer resources for the work assigned.

d. Establish and maintain communications with the associational missions committee and other appropriate groups.

(10) Personnel Committee

a. Survey the need for additional church staff positions.

b. Prepare and update as necessary position descriptions for all employed personnel.

c. Prepare and maintain an organizational manual relating to the church's employed personnel.

d. Recruit, interview, and recommend to the church new employed personnel. Exception: clerical and maintenance personnel are recruited, interviewed, and recommended for employment by the appropriate supervisor.

e. Develop and recommend salaries and benefits for employed personnel.

    f. Develop and recommend to the church policies and procedures for employed personnel administration.

(11) Preschool Committee
    a. Recommend and publicize policies and procedures.
    b. Recommend and purchase furnishings and supplies.
    c. Coordinate space assigned to preschool work.
    d. Work with church personnel committee to select, train, and supervise employed preschool workers.

(12) Weekday Education Committee
    a. Develop and recommend to the church policies and procedures for operating the program.
    b. Recommend to the personnel committee the employment, training, and supervision of personnel.
    c. Recommend the weekday education budget and the purchase of equipment.
    d. Serve as liaison between the church and the weekday education staff.
    e. See that the program complies with legal and licensing requirements.
    f. Make regular reports to the church.

(13) Public Relations Committee
    a. Determine within the church and community the understanding and acceptance of the church's work.
    b. Develop with organizational leaders a plan to interpret the church's work to its publics.
    c. Use appropriate media to communicate the church's work to its publics.
    d. Increase church member's awareness of the values of good church public relations.
    e. Recommend policies, procedures, and actions to improve church public relations.

(14) Ushering Committee
    a. Greet and seat people at services.
    b. Provide information about church services, programs, and building locations.
    c. Receive the offering, if assigned.
    d. Be attentive to the needs of persons during the services.

    e.   Restore the auditorium to physical orderliness after services.

(15) Audio Services Committee

    a.   Study and recommend the appropriate sound system.

    b.   Operate the sound system in consultation with the pastor and minister of music.

    c.   Provide a maintenance program for the upkeep of the equipment.

2. Duties of Church Officers

Church officers are elected by the church upon recommendation of the nominating committee. They serve for a three-year term and may succeed themselves.

(1) Moderator

    a.   Principal function: plan and conduct the church business meeting, and coordinate the work of church officers and committees.

    b.   The moderator is frequently the pastor. In the absence of the pastor, the chairman of the deacons may serve as the moderator.

(2) Trustees

    a.   Principal function: act as the legal agents of the church.

    b.   Members: three persons chosen from the church.

    c.   Term of office: Three years with one trustee's term expiring each year.

(3) Church Treasurer

    a.   Principal function: to assist in the receiving, accounting, and disbursing of all the church's monies.

    b.   Assistant(s) to the treasurer should be added as needed.

(4) Church Clerk

    a.   Principal function: to record and keep in permanent form all official actions of the church and to make this information available on request.

---

1. Ruth Ann Davies, *The School Library Media Center: a Force for Educational Excellence,* Second Edition (New York: R. R. Bowker, 1974), p. 21.

Chapter 12

Putting It Together with a Church Council

A church that ministers effectively in the complicated world of the eighties must learn to coordinate all its activities into one forward thrust for Christ. All the different programs must learn to work together for the benefit of the total body of Christ, the church. This is in keeping with the cherished principle of democracy by which Baptist churches have always done their work. The ministry of the church requires the full participation of the total people of God.

While final decision making rests with the entire congregation, most churches recognize that detailed planning and development of strategies must be done by representative planning groups. It would be impossible, for example, for every member of the church to study staff salaries and come to some agreement on a raise for the pastor and other paid staff members. This decision is a lot easier when it comes as a recommendation from a small group like the personnel committee, which has taken the time to study the matter thoroughly and draft a proposal for the church's approval.

One of the most important planning and recommending groups in a church is the church council. This group can help a church discover its reason for being and then guide it toward the fulfillment of its mission. Several questions about a church council serve to illustrate the role which it fills in a church's life.

THE CHURCH COUNCIL: WHAT IS IT?

The church council is a group of leaders, representing every area of the church's ministry, who meet regularly to plan, coordinate, and evaluate the church's work. This group has no power to make decisions for the church. It does study, analyze, and make proposals about the church's work. But the final decision on these matters rests with the church itself.

MEMBERSHIP OF THE CHURCH COUNCIL

Churches can make their own decisions about who serves on this planning group. But most congregations have discovered that the following church leaders are the logical ones who should form the church council.

1. Pastor

As the general leader and administrator of the church, the pastor serves on the church council. He usually serves as chairman of the group.

2. Church Staff Members

Some church staff members are responsible for assisting in the total development of one or more basic programs in the church, such as Sunday School or Woman's Missionary Union. A church staff worker whose responsibility is related to the entire operation of one or more of these basic programs should be a member of the church council.

3. Leaders of Basic Programs

There are six suggested basic programs for Southern Baptist churches: Sunday School, Church Training, music ministry, Woman's Missionary Union, Brotherhood, and pastoral ministries. Some churches have only two or three of these basic programs; others have all six. The directors of these basic programs are members of the church council.

4. Leaders of Service Programs

Two important organizations in a church are called service programs because they exist to help other church organizations do their work more effectively. These service organizations are media services and the church recreation ministry. The directors of these two organizations also serve on the church council.

5. Deacon Chairman

Deacons work with the pastor in a shepherding and pastoral

care ministry to church members. They also help cultivate and maintain the fellowship of the church. They should be represented on the church council by the chairman of deacons.

6. Chairmen of Key Committees
Most churches have a number of committees that request budget, calendar time, and personnel to do their work. These committees relate closely to the basic and service programs. Some of these committees are evangelism, missions, stewardship, and nominating. The chairman of these committees should definitely serve on the church council. The church may also direct that other important committees be represented.

DUTIES OF THE CHURCH COUNCIL

The duties of the church council are:
1. Help the church understand its mission and define its priorities.
2. Coordinate studies of church and community needs.
3. Recommend to the church coordinated plans for evangelism, missions, Christian development, worship, stewardship, and ministry.
4. Coordinate the church's schedule of activities, special events, and use of facilities.
5. Evaluate progress and the priority use of church resources.

THE FUNCTIONS OF THE CHURCH COUNCIL

The church council has a threefold job: to plan, coordinate, and evaluate the church's total program in order to help the church achieve a balanced ministry.

1. Planning
The only church which doesn't need to plan is the church that has unlimited time, money, and personnel to do everything that needs to be done in its local community. But few churches

are this fortunate. That's why churches need church councils to help them decide which ministries need to be provided immediately and which will have to be postponed until next year, or the next. This is a process of setting priorities, a harsh reality with which the church council must deal. In setting priorities, the church council should study what the Bible says about the nature and mission of the church and pay close attention to the needs of people in the church and its surrounding community.

After the church council sets priorities, church goals begin to emerge in the planning process. These goals state specifically what the church wants to accomplish—for whom, when, and where. Definite actions to help the church achieve these goals are called action plans. These action plans are usually assigned to programs or organizations represented on the church council.

For example, one church goal recommended by the church council might be to share the gospel with the lost. One way to do this would be to sponsor a Sunday School growth campaign. This action plan uses the Sunday School organization in outreach to non-Christians. The Sunday School director would be assigned the implementing of this action plan. He would work with the leaders of the Sunday School to complete this project.

2. Coordinating

Another job of the church council is to coordinate all the different elements of the church's ministry so they work together smoothly to accomplish church goals. There's no reason for two different programs to schedule meetings or ministries that conflict with each other if the church council is doing its job. It should use its meeting times to eliminate conflicts, overlaps, and duplication of effort among the various programs. This will assure a balanced program that moves the church toward the accomplishment of its goals.

One of the best examples of the coordinating work of a church council is a calendar of activities with all the major church events scheduled a year ahead of time. This prevents Church Training from scheduling a churchwide doctrinal study right in the middle of the annual spring revival. Problems like this are avoided when church council members sit down together and work on a yearly schedule for adoption by the church.

Coordination is basically teamwork. The church council itself must become a team before it can successfully coordinate the total work of the church into a productive whole.

3. Evaluating

Evaluation for the church council is a process of checking up on how the church is doing. After the completion of a major phase of the church's program, the church council should spend some time analyzing how it went and deciding how it might be done better the next time around. The church that refuses to evaluate its life and work is doomed to repeat its mistakes again and again. The church council can help prevent this by providing concise, evaluative reports on the church's ongoing program.

The evaluation process has several basic steps that church councils should learn to follow:

1. Set performance standards in advance to serve as the basis for future evaluation. These standards become the measuring rod for judging how well the church did.

2. Obtain accurate information continuously about the work that was performed.

3. Evaluate by comparing the actual performance with the standards that were set in advance.

4. Report evaluation to the congregation with suggestions for improvement or change.

Most church councils probably spend little time on evaluation because of the hours that planning and coordinating requires. But good evaluation may save planning time later on. It's an important part of a church council's work.

THE OFFICERS AND MEETINGS

To function effectively a church council needs some orderly principles and procedures of operation. These involve some officers and a regular meeting time.

1. Officers of the Church Council

The officers of a church council are a chairman and a secretary. The pastor usually serves as chairman, by virtue of his role as general leader of the church. The secretary is elected from among the group by other church council members. The church clerk or a church staff secretary might also be selected for this task.

Duties of the chairman.—The chairman of the church council is responsible to the church for leading the church council in the performance of its task. This involves the following specific duties:

1. Prepare and distribute an agenda for each meeting of the group.
2. Notify members of the time and place of each meeting.
3. Preside during the church council meeting.
4. Present plans and action suggestions to the church council.
5. Call for recommendations from the church council to the congregation during regular church business meetings.
6. Plan for training of church council members so they can perform their duties effectively.
7. Supervise the preparation and distribution of church council minutes, reports, and plans that are necessary to the proper operation of the group.

Duties of the secretary.—The secretary of the church council is responsible to the group, under the supervision of the chairman, for providing secretarial assistance required by the church council for the performance of its tasks. This involves the following duties:

1. Send an agenda for each meeting to members before each regular session of the group.
2. Notify council members of the time and place for each meeting.
3. Take minutes during meetings of the church council.
4. Distribute church council minutes, reports, and plans as directed by the chairman of the council.
5. Obtain records and other necessary facts requested by the church council.
6. Provide necessary supplies for use by the church council in its meetings.

164

2. Meetings of the Church Council

The church councils that are doing the most successful work usually meet monthly. Occasionally they also meet on call.

The pastor, as chairman, should outline the agenda and ask the secretary to mail each church council member a copy in advance. The agenda might include the following items:

1. Scripture reading, prayer
2. Approve agenda
3. Approve minutes of the last meeting
4. Report and evaluate church program activities
5. Receive pastor's report (on evangelism, for example)
6. Receive other reports as needed (from committee chairmen, for example)
7. Preview plans for the coming month
8. Prepare recommendations for the church
9. Assign duties to be completed before next meeting

HOW CAN A CHURCH START A CHURCH COUNCIL?

Churches use different procedures to start church councils. These steps might be helpful.

1. The pastor must realize what a church council can mean to the church and to his effectiveness as a leader. Talking with pastors of churches which have functioning church councils, attending conferences, and reading *Church Administration* magazine and other helpful materials will help the pastor recognize the advantages of having a church council in his own church.

2. Church leaders should be informed about the benefits of a church council.

3. A temporary study committee, appointed through usual procedures, might study the needs for a church council, outline its duties, and recommend that the church authorize the establishment of a church council. The recommendation might be either a resolution or an amendment to the church constitution.

4. The church should vote to authorize the establishment of a church council and approve its duties and functions.

Suggestions for the Teacher

Chapter 1

1. Write the title *A Church on Mission* on the chalkboard. Ask the members of the group what this title suggests about the work of the church in the world today.

2. Explain that chapter 1 of the book deals with biblical foundations for the church. Discuss briefly why it is important to begin a study of the church with this emphasis.

3. Write the phrase "Biblical Descriptions of the Church" on the chalkboard. Then ask the group to refer to their books to find all these descriptions of the church—such as "people of God"—enumerated in chapter 1. List all these phrases as they are discovered.

4. Ask, What truths do these descriptions reveal about the nature of the church and the work it should be doing in the world?

5. Divide the large group into three equal small groups. Group 1 should search chapter 1 for information on the intentions of a church. Group 2 should search for some biblical principles of church organization. Group 3 should study the discussion of church relationships. Let each group report on their findings.

Chapter 2

1. Before this session, write the phrase "The Needs of Persons" in capital letters at the top of the chalkboard. Ask the group, Why does a church have to be concerned about human needs?

2. Divide the chalkboard into two equal parts by drawing a line straight down the middle under the heading above. Print "Spiritual Needs" at the top of one column and "Other Needs" at the top of the other. Explain that this is how the writers organized chapter 2 of the book. Ask, Why is as much space devoted to spiritual needs as all the other human needs combined?

3. Ask members of the group to search chapter 2 and help you complete this chalkboard outline. List spiritual needs in the first column and other needs in the second.

4. Ask, Do you see any needs in both columns that might be closely related? How does God through Christ meet our deepest spiritual needs? What are some of the "other needs" of persons that a church can meet? What happens to people if their basic needs remain unresolved and unmet?

Chapter 3

1. Ask one person at least a week ahead of time to be prepared to present a report on "Life-changing Events of the Seventies" during this session.

2. After his presentation, ask other members of the group if they can recall other events from the seventies that had a profound influence on the way people live. List their recollections on the chalkboard.

3. Remind the group that it's always easier to look back on the past than to try to guess what will happen in the future. But ask them to name some of the projected issues and problems of the eighties they remember reading about in chapter 3 of the book. List their recollections on the chalkboard. Ask the group to supplement this list with their own ideas of what the critical issues and problems of the eighties will be.

4. Direct a brainstorming session about specific actions the church can take to meet the critical issues of the eighties. Another approach would be to break the large groups into smaller groups for more intense discussions. Let each group report its recommendations.

Chapter 4

1. Enlist three members of your group to serve on a panel during this session to discuss evangelism, family ministry, and Christian discipleship. Instruct them to read chapter 4 carefully and to be prepared to speak briefly on these three vital church concerns.

2. After this panel presentation, encourage members of the group to ask questions about these church concerns. Be prepared to generate discussion with questions like these: (1) Why do you think these three vital issues have surfaced as priority concerns in most churches today? (2) Are churches as concerned about lost

people today as they were thirty years ago? (3) Which of these three issues should be the top priorities of our own church?

3. Ask a member of the church staff to report briefly on the different programs and ministries already being provided by your own church which speak to these three vital issues. Let him or her serve as a resource person while your group brainstorms about other approaches that might be used to win people, minister to families, and train church members in Christian discipleship.

Chapter 5

1. Ask a member of the group to do a selective study of the book of Acts, looking for examples of how the New Testament church was empowered for its work by the Holy Spirit. Let this person bring a brief report on his findings, reading two or three key passages from Acts.

2. Ask, Why was the presence and power of the Holy Spirit essential to the work of the early church? Does the church today still need the empowering presence of the Spirit as much as the early church did?

3. Write the phrase "Functions of a Church" on the chalkboard. Under this heading write: (1) "Worship," (2) "Proclaim and Witness," (3) "Nurture and Educate," and (4) "Minister." Explain that these are continuing activities by which a church expresses its essential nature as the called-out people of God. Ask members of the group to think of specific church activities that demonstrate each of these broad functions of a church. List their comments on the chalkboard.

4. Divide the chalkboard into three sections. At the top of the sections write these headings: "Basic Church Programs," "Service Programs," "Emphasis Programs." Ask the members of the group to search through chapter 5 and find the specific church programs that should be listed under each of these headings.

5. After these lists are completed, discuss these different programs—their similarities and differences—in your own church. What can be done to make them even more effective in their unique ministries?

Chapter 6

1. Write this phrase "Pastoral Ministries: Leading the Church" on the chalkboard. Explain that pastoral ministries describes the work of the pastor, other church staff members, and deacons—those who are charged with the general responsibility of leading the church.

2. Ask members of the group to turn to 1 Timothy 3:1-13 in their Bibles. Explain that this passage deals with the qualifications of these key church leaders—pastor, deacons, and church staff members. Ask someone to read the passage aloud. Ask, What qualities do pastors, deacons, and church staff members need? What do these standards imply about the nature of their leadership role in the church?

3. Write the phrase "Tasks of the Pastoral Ministries Program" on the chalkboard. Explain that pastors, deacons, and church staff members are responsible for accomplishing four specific tasks in the church. Ask members of the group to search the last section of chapter 6 to locate these tasks. Write them on the chalkboard as they are located.

4. Ask, If you had to eliminate three of these tasks and keep only one, which would you retain? Which, in your opinion, is the most important task of pastoral ministries?

5. If the leadership task is mentioned, remind the group that pastoral ministries is to lead the church—not serve as the church itself.

Chapter 7

1. Ask two members of the group ahead of time to give their personal testimony on "What Sunday School Means to Me." After these formal presentations, ask other members of the group to tell about their positive experiences through Sunday School.

2. Tell the group, These personal statements are symbolic of how most Southern Baptists feel about the Sunday School. Why has Sunday School developed into such an important organization in most of our churches?

3. Then ask, What is one danger of a Sunday morning Bible study group that grows close and supportive across several

months until it reaches the point where the members really enjoy each other's company? What task of the Bible teaching program serves as a corrective for a situation like this?

4. After the outreach or witnessing task of the Bible teaching program is mentioned, lead members of the group to name the other tasks. Write them on the chalkboard as they are identified.

5. Remind the group that the heart of the Sunday School's work is reaching people and teaching the Bible. Close with a brainstorming session about how the teachers and Sunday School classes in your own church could teach the Bible more effectively.

Chapter 8

1. Prepare a poster with this heading, "Words for Growing Christians." Under this heading write the words: "Discipleship," "Maturity," "Gifts," "Learning," "Fully Equipped," "Upbuilding." Put the poster up and remind the group members that these are some key words you will be studying in this session. They are some of the major goals of the Church Training program of the church, discussed in chapter 8.

2. Ask members of the group to find Ephesians 4:11-16 in their Bibles. Let them read these verses silently and underline or circle every word that relates to the theme of Christian growth and discipleship. If some new words that imply Christian growth are discovered, list them on the poster.

3. Ask, Why is it so important that we continue to grow as Christians? What are some of the things that help a Christian grow?

4. Remind the group that the Church Training program of a church is designed to help Christians continue to grow and develop in their faith. Ask, What are some things you have learned through Church Training that have helped you grow as a Christian?

5. Write the four tasks of the Church Training program on the chalkboard. Divide the large group into small buzz groups of two or three people each and let them discuss the different ways in which these tasks help the church equip its members for Christian living and Christian ministry.

Chapter 9

1. Prepare a poster with this heading "Missions—Beyond Ourselves." Under this heading write these four phrases: "Woman's Missionary Union," "Brotherhood," "Establishing New Churches," and "Stewardship."

2. Ask one member of the group to examine your church's budget for this year and determine how much the congregation is giving to missions—all those causes beyond its own immediate needs. Ask him or her to determine what percentage of the total budget this amount represents and report it to the rest of the group. After this report, let the group discuss whether the amount going to missions is adequate.

3. If your church has a missions committee, ask the chairman of that committee to visit your group and discuss some of the mission projects your church is sponsoring in the local community. Ask the chairman about any plans this group might have to establish new missions and churches in your area.

4. Explain that the two missions education organizations in Southern Baptist churches are the Woman's Missionary Union and the Brotherhood organizations. Write on the chalkboard two columns with the headings "Tasks of the Woman's Missionary Union Program" and "Tasks of the Brotherhood Program." Lead members of the group in a search through chapter 9 to locate these tasks. Write them on the chalkboard as they are discussed.

5. Wrap up your discussion with this question: Why is it important for a church to reach beyond its own fellowship and express the love of Christ for all people everywhere?

Chapter 10

1. Ask members of the group to name their favorite hymns. Write the titles on the chalkboard as they are called out. Then explain that these hymn titles represent something of the diversity that the music ministry of a church must have. The music of a church must express the faith of a diverse and homogeneous congregation without degenerating into the lowest common denominator of music taste.

2. Ask four persons in advance to bring brief reports from chapter 10 on how the music ministry contributes to the growth

171

and spiritual development of the various age levels of the congregation—preschoolers, children, youth, and adults. Let them present these reports in panel fashion. Then lead your group in a general discussion of the ideas presented by the panel.

3. Ask members of the group to search chapter 10 to find the four tasks of the music ministry program. Write these tasks on the chalkboard as they are discovered.

4. Divide the large group into three equal small groups. Assign one of the first three tasks of the music ministry program to each of these groups. Ask them to discuss these tasks in light of how the music ministry of your church is performing them. They might want to make suggestions about additional projects that the music ministry in your church could perform. Ask the minister of music or some other leader in the music ministry in the church to be present to serve as a resource person.

Chapter 11

1. Prepare a poster with this heading, "Service Programs in a Church." Under the heading, write: (1) "Media Services," (2) "Recreation Services," and (3) "Administrative Services."

2. Enlist three members from your group ahead of time to read chapter 11 thoroughly and prepare brief reports on these three service programs. Let each one tell how one of these service programs can help a church do its work and achieve its mission. Give these assignments to members of your group who are working in these service programs, if possible.

3. After these presentations, lead the entire group in a general discussion of these service programs and the roles they fill in a church. Be prepared to keep the discussion going with questions like these: (1) Why do churches today need to be more media conscious than they have ever been? (2) How can media be used more effectively in witnessing to the lost? (3) Why should a church be concerned about how people spend their recreational and leisuretime? (4) How can recreation improve the fellowship of a church? (5) If a Baptist church is a democracy, why does it need church committees and church officers to handle specific jobs? (6) Name some key committees in our own church that

172

handle some important administrative services to enable the church to do its work.

Chapter 12

1. Ask the group, What would happen if we tried to plan the activities and programs of our church during the once-a-month business meeting on Wednesday night? Explain that it's impossible for the total church body to do detailed planning. That why every church needs a church council.

2. Write this phrase "The Church Council: What Is It?" on the chalkboard. Ask members of the group to find the definition in chapter 12. Write the definition on the chalkboard.

3. Lead the group in a discussion of various church leaders who serve on the church council. Ask, Why do you think these particular leaders of the church are singled out to serve on this group?

4. Write this phrase "Work of the Church Council" on the chalkboard. Mark off the chalkboard under the heading into three equal columns. Write "Planning," "Coordinating," and "Evaluating" at the top of these columns.

5. Ask members of the group to read the section "The Functions of the Church Council." Then ask, Why does a church need to plan, coordinate, and evaluate? Write their reasons in the appropriate columns on the chalkboard.

Personal Learning Activities

Chapter 1

1. What is the Greek word for church in the New Testament? What does this word mean?

2. What symbol or word picture does the apostle Paul most often use to describe the church?

3. According to the New Testament, what should be the three intentions or objectives of a church?

Chapter 2

4. List some of the meanings of the biblical teaching that man is created in the image of God.

5. God's ultimate purpose for redeemed humanity is _____ _____ _____ with others.

6. List some of the physiological needs of human beings.

7. How can a church help meet the universal need of people to belong to a group and to feel accepted?

Chapter 3

8. One of every _____ church members must serve as a leader to enable it to do its work.

9. What changes may the energy shortage bring about in churches during the eighties?

10. What are some changes that must take place in the churches before they can do a better job of winning the lost?

11. In your opinion, what are the three or four most critical problems that the church msut grapple with during the eighties?

Chapter 4

T2. Why is evangelism a priority concern of Southern Baptist churches?

13. List the resources that are available to help a church equip its members to witness.

14. What are some of the common needs of a couple during the newlywed years?

15. How should discipleship and evangelism be related in the life of a church?

16. Why does a Christian need a sound doctrinal understanding of the Christian faith?

Chapter 5
17. Why does a church need to make sure it does its work in the power of the Holy Spirit?

18. The four functions of a church are: (1) _____ , (2) _____ _____ and _____ , (3) _____ and _____ , (4) _____ _____ .

19. "Equip church leaders for service" is a task of what program of a church?

20. What are the three service programs of a church?

Chapter 6
21. Who are the people who serve in the pastoral ministries of a church?

22. The biblical model for pastor-deacon relationships in pastoral ministries is found in _____ .

23. What are the four tasks of pastoral ministries?

24. List several ways in which the gospel may be proclaimed by a church.

Chapter 7
25. Two examples of short-term noncontinuing Bible study in a church are _____ _____ _____ and _____ _____ _____ .

26. What are some techniques that a Sunday School class or department can use to reach people for Bible study?

27. Why is the Sunday School such an important organization in most churches?

28. How does the Sunday School lead church members to apply the truths of the Bible to their daily lives?

Chapter 8
29. The major themes of Christian discipleship are set forth in what passage of Scripture?

30. Why should new Christians get involved immediately in a program of growth in Christian discipleship?

31. What are the four content areas of the Church Training program's teaching task (task 2)?

32. _____ are given to enable us to contribute to the growth of other Christians.

Chapter 9

33. What are some of the broad, inclusive meanings of Christian stewardship?

34. What is the purpose of a stewardship committee?

35. List some things a missions committee can do to prepare the church to launch a new church or mission.

36. Define *mission action*.

37. "Support missions" is one of the tasks of the Woman's Missionary Union program. Name some specific projects this organization sponsors to support missions.

38. What are the five tasks of the Brotherhood program?

Chapter 10

39. What contribution can music make to the spiritual growth and personal development of a preschool child?

40. List the tasks of the music ministry program in a church.

41. How can a church use music groups and music presentations to reach more people for Christ?

Chapter 11

42. List the different types of materials included and cataloged in a church's media center.

43. Define *leisure*.

44. What are some Christian themes that can be explored creatively through church drama?

45. Name some positive values that can be communicated and reenforced through church-sponsored retreats.

46. Why does a church need administrative services?

Chapter 12

47. List the leaders who serve on the church council.

48. Name the duties of the chairman of the church council.

49. The threefold job of the church council is to _____ , _____ , and _____ the church's total program in order to help the church achieve a balanced ministry.